DRUGS
your questions answered
A READER FOR STUDENTS

ISDD is here to advance knowledge, understanding and policy making about drugs

Published by
ISDD (Institute for the Study of Drug Dependence)
Waterbridge House
32-36 Loman Street
London SE1 OEE
Tel: 0171 928 1211
Fax: 0171 928 1771

ISBN: 0 948830 33 6

Edited by Ross Coomber & Harry Shapiro
Sub-edited by Oswin Baker
Designed and typeset by Jan Hodgman
Cover by Andrew Haig Associates

Produced in association with the Department of Health

Contents page

Introduction

This book is aimed at all students doing projects or dissertations on drug misuse from A-level upwards including those at college, university or doing pre-vocational or in-service training.

The ISDD information service receives hundreds of enquiries from students every year, many of whom ask for literature to answer the same questions about the misuse of drugs such as 'Should drugs be legalised?' or 'How many drug users are there?' What we have done is to bring together articles and extracts from books which help to answer some of the most popular questions. Obviously no one article can give you the complete picture on any given topic, so at the end we have included a list of further readings on each of the topics covered in the book.

You are welcome to use the ISDD information service. We take enquiries by phone, letter or fax and you can come to the library by appointment between 10am-4.30pm Monday to Friday. We also sell a comprehensive range of publications. Please ask for a catalogue.

Illicit drugs and their effects

by Harry Shapiro

Introduction

The reader should bear in mind that the information given here is only a summary, and that the use of drugs for non-medical purposes is a little understood aspect of human behaviour. Drug effects are strongly influenced by the amount taken, the surroundings, and the reactions of other people – let alone the mental and physical state of the user. All these influences are themselves tied up with social and cultural attitudes to and beliefs about drugs, as well as more general social conditions. So it is generally misleading to make simple cause-and-effect statements, such as 'drug X always causes condition Y'.

This article deals only with illicit 'street' drugs and includes solvents which, although not illicit as such, when used for recreational purposes, are certainly disapproved of in society. This article does not deal either with drugs like alcohol, tobacco or tranquillisers although clearly there are major health implications associated with their heavy use. A minority of tranquilliser users will be street drug users who inject a tranquilliser in gel form called temazepam.

Readers may have heard of some exotic drugs like GHB and Ketamine. Many of these are fashionable for only a short time and then disappear – it is too early to say whether they will join the legal high of 'poppers'. However for more information on these or other drugs not covered in this article, please contact the ISDD information service.

Drug terms

Tolerance refers to the way the body gets used to the repeated presence of a drug. It means that higher doses are needed to maintain the same effect.

Adapted from *Drug Abuse Briefing 5*. Available from ISDD

Withdrawal effects are the body's reaction to the sudden absence of a drug to which it has adapted. The effects can be overcome by taking more of the drug, or by 'cold turkey' – rapid withdrawal which may last up to a week.

Dependence describes a compulsion to continue taking a drug in order to feel good or to avoid feeling bad. When this is done to avoid the physical discomfort of withdrawal, we speak of *physical dependence. Psychological dependence* describes the use of drugs as an emotional 'crutch' giving stimulation, pleasure or an escape from reality. It is recognised as the most widespread and most important of the two.

Addiction implies that a drug dependency has developed to such an extent that it has serious detrimental effects on the user. They may be chronically intoxicated, have great difficulty stopping the drug use, and be determined to obtain the drug by almost any means. The term is inextricably linked to society's reaction to the user, and so medical experts now generally avoid it as it carries too many non-medical connotations.

The term **problem drug use** refers to drug use resulting in social, psychological, physical or legal problems associated with dependence, intoxication or regular excessive consumption. In other words, it is not necessarily the frequency of drug use which is the primary 'problem', but the effects that drug-taking has on the user's life.

Drug 'abuse' and **drug 'misuse'** are terms that are hard to pin down. Essentially they indicate the belief that taking a drug is harmful (abuse) or that its use is socially unacceptable (misuse). Authorised medical use is by definition acceptable and not harmful and so both terms overlap with the less subjective phrase, *non-medical use*. People who take drugs usually refer to themselves as 'using' drugs or as 'users'.

Drug laws

Under each drug in the paragraphs below on legal status, mention is made of the Medicines Act 1968 and the Misuse of Drugs Act 1971. These are the two main UK laws about drugs. The first governs the manufacture and supply of medicinal products of all kinds, whilst the aim of the second is to prevent the non-medical use of certain drugs.

Drugs controlled under the Misuse of Drugs Act are placed in different classes, depending on the penalties associated with offences involving that drug: class A have the highest penalties, class C the lowest. For all these drugs it is an offence to possess them or to supply them to someone else without legal authority. These drugs are usually only legally available on prescription.

Allowing anyone on your premises to produce or to supply (give away or sell) illegal drugs is an offence. It is an offence even if they only offer to supply the drug. It is an offence if one or both parents know about, but do nothing to prevent, their son or daughter from sharing illegal drugs with a friend in their house. It is an offence to permit the smoking of cannabis or opium in your house. To supply or offer to supply any article, except syringes and needles, believing that it will be used to prepare controlled drugs or to administer them (to yourself or others) in an illegal context is also an offence.

Maximum sentences for breaking the Misuse of Drugs Act are severe. First offenders who are charged with the possession of drugs which are for their own use, are likely to get off with a caution. However, others may be fined which means a criminal record, and regular offenders, people selling drugs, or drug smugglers, might well be imprisoned. The maximum penalty for trafficking offences is life imprisonment.

If someone finds what they think is an illegal drug, they must hand it without delay to someone authorised to possess illegal drugs, usually a police officer. To prevent another person committing an offence with a drug, you can either destroy it or hand it to the police.

Drugtaking and risk-taking

Most people who use drugs come to no harm, but there are some very serious dangers which apply across all drug types:

Overdoing it

Taking too much in one go risks an experience that gets out of control and causes distress or even fatal overdose. Obviously, the more that is taken, the higher the risk of intoxication.

If anyone takes a psychoactive drug (meaning a drug which affects the mind) in high doses over a long period, it is likely to distort their perception of and response to their environment. This could impair their normal physical functioning and development.

As tolerance and dependence develop, the problems of financing drug purchases can add to the deterioration of diet, housing and lifestyle.

Wrong time, wrong place

Even in moderate doses most psychoactive drugs impair motor control, reaction time, and attention span. These effects can last several hours. No matter how the person feels, they are not as capable as before. When driving, operating machinery or crossing roads they become more dangerous to themselves and to others.

Many drugs amplify mood. So if someone is depressed, anxious or aggressive, drugs can make things a lot worse. Even drugs which are thought of as calming (like alcohol and tranquillisers) can release aggressive impulses because they weaken social and personal inhibitions.

Individual differences

Statements about drug effects are often either about what might happen in extreme cases, or about what usually happens with most people. But not everyone is 'usual'. For instance, some people develop a toxic reaction to a single cup of coffee. Individuals with psychotic tendencies may be 'pushed over the brink' by their experiences under the influence of powerful hallucinogens like LSD. Drug effects also vary with body weight. In general, less heavy people are more affected than heavier people on the same dose.

Adulteration and mistaken identity

Drugs offered on the illicit market are often not what they are claimed to be. If illicitly manufactured, they are likely to contain impurities or adulterants. The buyer can never be sure how strong the substance is. This adds greatly to the unpredictability of the effects of drugs obtained either without medical supervision or the quality control which is imposed on licit manufacturers.

Doubling up

The dangers of any drug are likely to be increased if it is taken while another drug is still in the body. Doubling up on depressant drugs (alcohol, solvents, opiates, tranquillisers) is probably the most dangerous. Complex interactions can occur between other types of drugs, and loading one drug on top of another multiplies the risk.

Pregnancy

There are two major ways in which drugs might damage a foetus.

Firstly, heavy use may affect the mother's health either directly or through self-neglect and poor nutrition.

Secondly, drugs may reach the foetus through the mother's bloodstream and its immature bodily processes are less able to cope than those of an adult. These risks are by no means the same for all drugs, and are best understood for drugs with depressant effects.

In general heavy drug use in pregnancy is associated – probably for a variety of reasons – with premature birth and low birth weight. There is also an increased risk of the baby dying around the time of birth. On the other hand, research on the effects of moderate drug use is generally inconclusive and many heavy drug users give birth to perfectly healthy babies. But this is an under-researched area, and doctors generally advise pregnant women not to take drugs if it can be avoided.

Injection

Injection is the least widespread method of taking drugs and is also the most hazardous. When injected, the drug obviously enters the bloodstream immediately and some is carried directly to the brain, producing an effect within seconds. For this reason all the effects of the drug are more intense, the user is incapacitated more quickly and the risks become more serious.

HIV and hepatitis can be introduced through sharing blood-contaminated, non-sterile syringes or needles. Those who are HIV positive can go on to develop AIDS. Those infected with HIV may not have any symptoms, and may not develop AIDS for several years, or possibly not at all. From the moment they are infected, however, they carry the virus in their blood, and can infect other people through sexual intercourse and sharing injecting equipment.

Other major dangers arising from injecting are overdose, abscesses, septicaemia, gangrene and damage from using crushed tablets and other dosage forms not meant to be injected. When a drug is injected dependence is more likely for three reasons: high doses are common, drug users enjoy the 'rush', and the injection ritual may become as important to the user as the effects of the drug itself. Nevertheless dependence is not inevitable and takes time to develop.

The drugs

Amphetamines

Amphetamines are synthetic powders which are available as a variety of tablets, capsules etc sometimes in combination with other drugs. These have a medical use and in the 1950s and 1960s they were widely prescribed for depression and to suppress appetite. They are now only recommended for the treatment of pathological sleepiness and (paradoxically) hyperactivity in children. Amphetamines may be swallowed in tablet form, or sniffed, smoked, or injected as a powder.

Legal status

All amphetamines and similar stimulants are 'prescription only' drugs under the Medicines Act. With the exception of some milder stimulants they are also controlled under the Misuse of Drugs Act as a class B drug, but as Class A if prepared for injection. Doctors can still supply them and patients can possess them when they have been prescribed. Apart from this their production, supply and possession are offences. Allowing premises to be used for their production or supply is also an offence.

Prevalence and availability

Street amphetamine is usually illicitly manufactured amphetamine sulphate powder.

Illicit amphetamine is heavily cut (often to less than five per cent purity) and sells for around £10-£15 per gram. An occasional user might take a few weeks to consume ½ gram. A heavy user who has developed substantial tolerance might consume several grams a day of relatively impure amphetamine.

Short-term use

Amphetamines arouse and activate the user much as the body's natural adrenalin does. Breathing and heart rate speed up, the pupils widen, and appetite lessens. The user feels more energetic, confident and cheerful. Because of these effects, there is a risk of psychological dependence.

As the body's energy stores become depleted, the predominant feelings may become anxiety, irritability and restlessness. High doses – especially if frequently repeated over several days – can produce delirium, panic, hallucinations and feelings of persecution.

The effects of a single dose last about three to four hours and leave the user feeling tired. It can take a couple of days for the body to fully recover.

Long-term use

To maintain the desired effects, the regular user has to take increasing doses, often many times the normal dose. When they eventually stop, they are likely to feel depressed, lethargic and ravenously hungry. Amphetamines merely postpone fatigue and hunger and do not satisfy the need for rest and nourishment. Heavy use also risks damaged blood vessels or heart failure. This is especially true for people with high blood pressure or pulse rates and people (like athletes) who take strenuous exercise while using the drug.

Regular high dosage users are liable to develop delusions, hallucinations and paranoia. Sometimes these develop into a psychotic state, from which it can take several months to fully recover. Heavy use also debilitates the user due to lack of sleep and food and lowers resistance to disease, all of which can have serious effects on health.

Cannabis

Cannabis derives from *Cannabis sativa*, a bushy plant easily cultivated in Britain. It is generally used as a relaxant and a mild intoxicant. The most important active ingredients are concentrated in the resin at the top of the plant. 'Hashish' or 'hash' is resin scraped from the plant and compressed into blocks. It is the commonest form in the UK. Herbal cannabis (grass) is a weaker preparation of the dried plant material. Increasingly however, stronger 'designer' forms of herbal cannabis are being grown in this country from seeds imported from Europe (eg, 'skunk', 'northern lights'). Less common in the UK and strongest of all, is cannabis oil, a liquid prepared from the resin.

In the UK cannabis is prepared into 'joints' or 'spliffs' and smoked often in combination with tobacco. Cannabis can also be smoked in a pipe, brewed as a drink, or cooked with.

Legal status

Cannabis is strictly controlled under the Misuse of Drugs Act, and is a class B drug. It is illegal to cultivate, produce, supply or possess, unless a Home Office licence has been issued for research or other special purposes. It is also an offence to allow premises to be used for cultivating, producing, supplying or smoking cannabis.

Prevalence and availability

Cannabis has the greatest non-medical usage of all the drugs controlled under the Misuse of Drugs Act. It is now established in the leisure activity of large sections of the population – latest surveys suggest that perhaps eight million people have tried the drug.

At 'street' level, imported herbal cannabis retails for about £50-80 an ounce, resin for £14-25 per ¼ ounce. Eaten, £1.50's worth of resin would be sufficient to produce the desired effects. Smoked, about the same or slightly less could be used to make a couple of cannabis cigarettes sufficient for two or three people to get mildly intoxicated. Recreational users might consume an eighth of an ounce per week; heavy and regular cannabis users, that amount in a day.

Short-term use

Effects depend largely on the expectations, motivations, and mood of the user, the amount used and the situation. Most people do not experience very much at first and have to learn which effects to look out for.

The most common and also the most sought-after effects are talkativeness, bouts of hilarity, relaxation and greater appreciation of sound and colour. While intoxicated, the cannabis smoker will be less able to perform tasks requiring concentration or intellectual or manual dexterity. Some of these effects can be reduced if they concentrate.

There may be perceptual distortion with higher doses. People who use the drug when anxious or depressed, may find that their unpleasant feelings are magnified, and sometimes experience short-term panic. The same is true of inexperienced people using high doses. There is virtually no danger of fatal overdose.

The effects generally start a few minutes after smoking, and may last up to one hour with low doses and for several hours with high doses. There is no hangover of the type associated with alcohol.

Long-term use

For the vast majority of users, there is no conclusive evidence that long-term cannabis use causes lasting damage to physical or mental health. However – as with tobacco – frequently inhaled cannabis smoke probably causes bronchitis and other respiratory disorders, and may cause lung cancer. Cannabis may therefore cause special risks for people with lung, respiratory or heart disorders. Heavy use in people with disturbed personalities can precipitate a temporary psychiatric disorder.

Cannabis does not seem to produce physical dependence. Regular users can, however, come to feel a psychological need for the drug or may rely on it as a 'social lubricant'. As with other sedating drugs people chronically intoxicated on cannabis may appear apathetic, sluggish and neglect their appearance but there is no evidence of a special cannabis 'amotivational syndrome'.

Cocaine

Cocaine is a white powder derived from the leaves of the Andean coca shrub, with powerful stimulant properties similar to those of amphetamine. It is commonly sniffed or 'snorted' up the nose through a tube and absorbed into the blood supply via the nasal membranes. It is also injected and smoked, the smokable variety being known as crack.

Legal status

Cocaine, its various salts, and the leaves of the coca plant, are controlled in class A of the Misuse of Drugs Act. Cocaine can still be prescribed, but otherwise it is illegal to produce, possess or supply it. It is also illegal to allow premises to be used for producing or supplying the drug.

Prevalence and availability

Cocaine and crack use appears to be on the increase in the UK. The powder costs around £85-£100 for a gram of 50 per cent pure drug. Although sold in small 'rocks' (about raisin size) at about £25 per rock, crack costs about the same per gram, but can be anything to 100 per cent pure. The intermittent user might sniff ¼ to ½ gram of powder over two or three days. Regular crack users with sufficient supplies might consume several grams a day.

Short-term use

Like amphetamine, cocaine produces physiological arousal accompanied by exhilaration,decreased hunger, indifference to pain and fatigue, and feelings of great physical strength and mental capacity. Sometimes these desired effects are replaced by anxiety or panic. When sniffed, the psychological effects peak after about 15 to 30 minutes and then diminish. This means the dose may have to be repeated every 20 minutes to maintain the effect. When smoked, the effects are felt more immediately and wear off more quickly.

Large doses or a 'spree' of quickly repeated doses can lead to an extreme state of agitation, anxiety, paranoia and, perhaps, hallucination. These effects generally fade as the drug is eliminated from the body. The after-effects of cocaine include fatigue and depression. Excessive doses can cause death from respiratory or heart failure, but these are rare.

Long-term use

There are no clear cut tolerance effects with cocaine. Nor are there withdrawal effects of the kind that require the user to continue taking the drug to avoid feeling ill. However, cocaine users may develop a strong psychological dependence on the feelings of physical and mental wellbeing it affords and are often tempted to step up the dose. After discontinuing the user will feel fatigued, sleepy and depressed, all of which reinforce the temptation to repeat the dose.

With heavy and frequent use, increasingly unpleasant symptoms develop. Euphoria is replaced by an uncomfortable state of restlessness, hyperexcitability, nausea, insomnia and weight loss. These generally persuade people to cut down or stop for a while. Continued use may lead to a state of mind similar to paranoid psychosis. Regular users may appear chronically nervous, excitable and paranoid. All these effects generally clear up once use is discontinued. Repeated sniffing can damage the membranes lining the nose and may also damage the structure separating the nostrils. Prolonged smoking may cause a number of respiratory problems.

Ecstasy

Ecstasy or MDMA is classed as a hallucinogenic amphetamine, a group of drugs with effects roughly combining those of amphetamines and LSD.

Legal status

Ecstasy is a class A drug. No doctor can prescribe it and anybody wanting to use it for research purposes has to obtain a licence from the Home Office.

Prevalence and availability

Ecstasy has been available in this country since the mid-eighties, but only in any quantity since 1988 when it became strongly associated with Acid House music and the 'raves' at which it was played. Since then, use of the drug has become more widespread among young people not necessarily connected with the music scene. The drug is sold in a wide variety of capsules and tablets of differing shapes and colours for anything between £10-£25 a tablet. As the drug has become more popular, so the 'quality' has decreased – many tablets and capsules sold as ecstasy may not contain any active drug at all or are a mixture of other drugs.

Short-term use

MDMA is effective at the moderate single dose level of 75-100mg. Effects are experienced after 20-60 minutes and can last several hours. Pupils become dilated, the jaw tightens and there is usually brief nausea, sweating, dry mouth and throat, a rise in blood pressure and pulse rates, and loss of appetite. There can be some difficulty with bodily coordination making it dangerous to drive or operate machinery. At doses above 200mg or if the drug is being used repeatedly over a few days, all these effects may be experienced more acutely. Once the drug has worn off, there may be some residual effects similar to those experienced by amphetamine users including fatigue and depression which can last for several days.

As with LSD, whether the experience is 'bad' or 'good' often depends on the mood and expectations of the user. At moderate levels most users report a mild euphoric 'rush' followed by feelings of serenity and calmness and the dissipation of anger and hostility. Most of the bad experiences with the drug have been reported by those using higher doses over a period of time and include anxiety, panic, confusion, insomnia, psychosis, and visual and auditory hallucinations. Generally, these effects die down once the drug is stopped, but can leave the user in a weakened mental and physical condition for a while. Some of these effects have been experienced by those who have tried the drug for 'self-therapy' and have then been unable to deal with the emotions that using MDMA has brought to the surface.

So far around 50 deaths directly associated with the effects of taking ecstasy have been recorded in otherwise apparently healthy young people. All these young people collapsed at raves or shortly afterwards and all exhibited symptoms associated with severe heatstroke. The current best guess is that these users have succumbed to the cumulative effects of taking MDMA while dancing for long periods in a very hot, humid atmosphere.

Long-term use

There is evidence from research carried out by the National Poisons Unit of an association between ecstasy use and liver damage. Tolerance develops to the effects of MDMA, but there is no physical dependence, no heroin-like withdrawal symptoms nor any evidence that MDMA is used compulsively for years.

Overall, the literature suggests that people should not take MDMA if they suffer from heart disease, high blood pressure, glaucoma, epilepsy or are in poor physical or mental condition. Women with a history of genito-urinary tract infection should not use the drug. There is no evidence that the drug has any effect on the foetus or causes problems in the newborn.

Heroin and other opiates

Opiates are drugs derived from the opium poppy. Opium is the dried 'milk' of the poppy and contains morphine and codeine. From morphine it is not difficult to produce heroin which is, in pure form, a white powder over twice as potent as morphine. Opiates have medical uses as painkillers, cough suppressants and anti-diarrhoea treatments.

A number of synthetic opiates are manufactured as painkillers. These include pethidine, dipipanone (Diconal), dextropropoxyphene (Distalgesic) and methadone (Physeptone), a drug often prescribed for opiate addiction.

Opiate powders can be swallowed, or dissolved in water and injected. Heroin can be sniffed up the nose like cocaine, or smoked by heating it and inhaling the fumes ('chasing the dragon').

Legal status

Opiates are controlled under the Misuse of Drugs Act. This makes it illegal to supply or to possess them without a prescription, or to produce, import or export them without authority. It is also an offence to allow premises to be used for producing or supplying these drugs. Only specially licensed doctors can prescribe heroin or dipipanone for the treatment of opiate addiction. All other opiates can be prescribed for normal therapeutic uses. Heroin, morphine, opium, and methadone are class A drugs.

Prevalence and availability

Since the late 1970s there has been an apparently rapid rise in heroin use and heroin dependence, both injecting and smoking. Doctors notify the Home Office of patients who are addicted to certain opiates and cocaine. During 1993 there were nearly 30,000 notified addicts, of whom a vast majority were addicted to heroin, but there are likely to be many thousands more who do not come forward for treatment.

Fifty per cent pure heroin sells for about £100 per gram, usually cut with a variety of powders of similar appearance, including glucose powder, caffeine, flour, talcum powder, and drug substances like phenobarbitone powder. An addict might use ¼ gram a day.

Short-term use

Moderate doses of pure opiates produce a range of generally mild physical effects (although the painkilling effect will be marked even at moderate doses). They depress the nervous system, including reflex functions such as coughing, respiration and heart rate. They also dilate blood vessels (giving a feeling of warmth) and depress bowel activity, resulting in constipation.

Low doses produce euphoria with sedation at higher doses and the chance of overdose where the user can go into a coma and possibly die from respiratory failure. Overdose is more likely if other depressant drugs, like alcohol, are used at the same time and there can be fatal reactions to injected adulterants.

Opiates induce a relaxed detachment from pain, desires and anxiety. They make people feel drowsy, warm and content, and relieve stress and discomfort. However, among people who have developed physical dependence and tolerance, positive pleasure is replaced by the relief of obtaining the drug, and they need it just to stay 'normal'.

Along with or instead of these reactions, first use (especially injection) often causes nausea and vomiting. These unpleasant reactions also quickly disappear with repeated doses. The effect of sniffing heroin is slower and less intense than that of intravenous injecting. The effects of heroin are felt as quickly after smoking as after intravenous injecting, but are not so intense.

Long-term use

As tolerance develops regular users increase the dose to achieve repeated euphoria. After several weeks on high doses, sudden withdrawal results in a variable degree of discomfort, comparable to flu. The effects start eight to twenty-four hours after the last dose and include aches, tremor, sweating, chills, sneezing, yawning and muscular spasms. They generally fade in seven to ten days, but feelings of weakness and loss of wellbeing last for several months. People can overdose when they take their usual 'fix' after a break during which tolerance has faded.

Physical dependence is not as significant as the strong psychological dependence developed by some long-term users. Dependence of any kind is not inevitable and some people use heroin on an occasional basis.

The physiological effects of long-term opiate use are rarely serious in themselves. But physical damage, associated largely with repeated, often unhygienic, injecting and with the injection of adulterants, is common among addicts. Injectors also run the risk of HIV/AIDS unless they always use sterile equipment. Repeated heroin sniffing can damage the membranes lining the nose. Also decreased appetite and apathy can contribute to illness caused by poor nutrition, self-neglect and bad housing. As tolerance and dependence develop, financial difficulties can also contribute to self-neglect and a diminished quality of life.

LSD

Lysergic acid diethylamide (LSD) is a synthetic white powder. The minute amounts sufficient for a 'trip' are generally mixed with other substances to make tablets or capsules to be swallowed. The drug is normally absorbed onto brightly patterned paper squares, and can be absorbed onto gelatin sheets or sugar cubes. The strength of all these preparations is uncertain.

Legal status

LSD and other hallucinogens are strictly controlled (class A) under the Misuse of Drugs Act. It is illegal to produce, supply or possess these drugs except in accordance with a Home Office licence issued for research or other special purposes. It is also an offence to allow premises to be used for the production or supply of these drugs.

Prevalence and availability

LSD use (often called 'trips') is quite common among young people in the drug scene. Tablets containing LSD (one or two of which are sufficient for a 'trip') cost £2-£3 each.

Short-term use

A trip begins about half an hour after taking LSD, peaks after two to six hours and fades out after about 12 hours, depending on the dose. It usually progresses through several phases. Experiences whilst on LSD are hard to describe. This is partly because they vary but also because they can be at variance with our accustomed view of the world.

Effects depend very much on the user's mood, the setting, who they are with as well as the dose. They often include intensified colours and visual or auditory distortions.

It is difficult to combine a 'trip' with a task requiring concentration, and driving will almost certainly be impaired.

Emotional reactions may include heightened self-awareness and mystical or ecstatic experiences. A feeling of being outside one's body is commonly reported. Physical effects are generally insignificant. Unpleasant reactions ('bad trips') may include depression, dizziness, disorientation and sometimes panic. These are more likely if the user is unstable, anxious, or depressed, or in hostile or unsuitable surroundings.

Deaths due to suicide or hallucinations, though much publicised, are rare. Only one fatal LSD overdose has been recorded.

Long-term use

There is no reliable evidence of physical damage from repeated use of LSD. The main hazards are psychological rather than physical. Serious anxiety or brief 'psychotic reactions' may occur, but can usually be dealt with by friendly reassurance. Prolonged serious adverse psychological reactions are rare. They are most likely in individuals with existing psychological difficulties.

Brief but vivid re-experiences of part of a previous trip have been reported, especially after frequent use. These can leave the person feeling disorientated and can be distressing, but are only very rarely dangerous.

There is no physical dependence, and the fact that for several days after taking LSD further doses are less effective discourages frequent use.

Hallucinogenic mushrooms

Several species of mushrooms can have hallucinogenic effects when eaten. About a dozen of these grow wild in the UK, notably the Liberty Cap. The Liberty Cap contains the hallucinogenic chemicals psilocybin and psilocin. They may be eaten fresh, cooked or brewed into a tea, and can be preserved by drying. Due to variations in potency, it is impossible to say how many are required for a hallucinogenic experience. It would seem that 20 to 30 is a usual dose but much fewer may suffice.

Distinguishing hallucinogenic mushrooms from poisonous (and possibly deadly) cousins is a complex skill, requiring knowledge of botany and expertise in mushroom classification.

Legal status

It is not illegal to pick and eat 'magic' mushrooms. However they contain psilocin or psilocybin which are Class A drugs. If anything is done to the mushrooms such as boiling or crushing them or even drying them out, the person could be accused of making a 'preparation or other product' containing psilocin or psilocybin and so charged with possessing a class A drug.

Prevalence and availability

The Liberty Cap seems the most commonly occurring and most commonly used of the available species. It is also the most consistently potent. It fruits between September and November. *Amanita muscaria* too is very common in early Autumn. However its unpleasant side-effects and the likelihood and dangers of mistaken identity reduce its use as a recreational drug.

Short-term use

The effects of psilocybin-containing mushrooms are similar to a mild LSD experience. However the effects come on more quickly and last for a shorter time. At low doses euphoria and detachment predominate. At higher doses visual distortions progress to vivid hallucinations. There are commonly feelings of nausea, vomiting and stomach pains.

'Bad trips' can occur and may develop into a psychotic episode. These are most common after repeated or unusually high doses, or if the user is inexperienced or anxious and unhappy. They can usually be dealt with by friendly reassurance.

There have been reports of longer lasting disturbances, such as anxiety attacks and 'flashbacks' to the original experience. These almost invariably fade of their own accord.

By far the greatest danger is the possibility of picking a poisonous mushroom by mistake.

Long-term use

Like LSD, tolerance rapidly develops and the next day it might take twice as many Liberty Caps to repeat the experience, which naturally discourages frequent use. There are no significant withdrawal symptoms and no physical dependence. Individuals may, however, feel a desire to repeat their experiences. No serious effects of long-term hallucinogenic mushroom use have been reported, but no studies have been undertaken which permit the effects of extended frequent use to be assessed.

Solvents

Some organic (carbon-based) substances produce effects similar to alcohol or anaesthetics when their vapours are inhaled. A number have applications as solvents (in glues, paints, nail varnish removers, dry cleaning fluids, de-greasing compounds etc). Others are used as propellant gases (in aerosols and fire extinguishers) or as fuels (petrol, cigarette lighter gas).

Sometimes sniffers heighten the effect by increasing the concentration of the vapour and/or excluding air, for instance by sniffing from inside a plastic bag placed over the head.

Legal status

Under the Intoxicating Substances (Supply) Act 1985 it is an offence to supply or offer to supply solvents to persons aged under 18 if the supplier has reason to believe that they intend to misuse them. In Scotland it is an offence to 'recklessly' sell solvents to children knowing they intend to inhale them. Other than this, selling, possessing or sniffing solvents as such is not restricted. Sniffers may be convicted for unruly, offensive or intoxicated behaviour or because they resist police attempts to intervene. Someone driving under the influence of solvents may be convicted of driving whilst unfit due to drink or drugs.

Prevalence and availability

Glues and most other 'sniffable' products are easily available in shops. The government has published guidelines for retailers advising that these products are stocked out of reach of children and that sales staff refuse to sell them to children whom they suspect may misuse them. Solvent misuse has always tended to be more popular among younger children as they cannot afford to buy drugs or are too young to go into pubs. However the recent fall in deaths from solvent misuse may mean that solvent misuse is becoming less fashionable as younger people have more access to drugs.

Short-term use

Inhaled solvent vapours are absorbed through the lungs and rapidly reach the brain. Part of the effect is due to reduced oxygen intake. Body functions like breathing and heart rate are depressed, and repeated or deep inhalation can result in an 'overdose' causing disorientation, loss of control, and unconsciousness from which in normal circumstances sniffers quickly recover. The experience is very like being drunk. Experienced sniffers may go on to seek dreamlike experiences. Generally these are not true hallucinations as youngsters don't confuse them with reality.

The effects of solvent vapours come on quickly, and disappear within a few minutes to half an hour if sniffing is stopped. Afterwards the user may experience a mild hangover (headaches, poor concentration) for about a day. Sniffers run the risk of accidental death or injury if they are 'drunk' in an unsafe environment, such as on a roof or by a canal bank. Sniffers could die from choking on vomit if they sniff to the point of unconsciousness. If the method used to inhale the solvent obstructs breathing (eg, large plastic bags placed over the head) and the sniffer becomes unconscious, death from suffocation may result.

Some products (notably aerosol gases and cleaning fluids) sensitise the heart and can cause heart failure, especially if sniffers exert themselves at the same time. Gases 'squirted' directly into the mouth can cause death from suffocation.

Long-term use

Very long-term (eg, ten years) heavy solvent misuse might result in moderate, lasting impairment of brain function, affecting especially the control of movement. Chronic misuse of aerosols and cleaning fluids has caused lasting kidney and liver damage. Repeatedly sniffing leaded petrol may result in lead poisoning.

Despite these possibilities, lasting damage attributable to solvent misuse seems extremely rare. In Britain, surveys of groups of sniffers have not revealed any persistent medical consequences.

While someone is sniffing repeatedly, the 'hangover' effects of pallor, fatigue, forgetfulness and loss of concentration can become a recurring daily pattern. This could affect their performance and functioning and there can be weight loss, depression and tremor. These symptoms will tend to clear up once sniffing is discontinued.

Tolerance develops, but physical dependence is not a significant problem. Psychological dependence develops in a minority of susceptible youngsters with underlying family or personality problems. These people will probably become 'lone sniffers' as opposed to the usual pattern of sniffing in groups.

Why People Use Drugs

by Martin Plant

A daunting number of suggestions have been put forward to explain why people use drugs and why some users become dependent on them. Many of these theories are speculative and anecdotal, stemming from personal experiences and observation of a few drugtakers rather than from rigorous research. Most theories about the *causes* of drug use or drug dependence rely upon descriptions of *established* drugtakers. There is very little information about the characteristics of these individuals before they become involved in drugs. For this reason there has been frequent confusion between the *causes* of drug use and its apparent *correlates* or even *consequences*.

Most British studies of drug users have been confined to highly selective groups such as students or people in treatment institutions. The significant differences noted between different groups such as heroin dependants in a clinic or cannabis smokers in a college have been largely responsible for the different causal theories put forward. Virtually every writer on the subject of drug use has ventured some opinion, but most have highlighted themes that are relevant to *their* particular study group of drugtakers and which may have little relevance to others. While a perplexing number of equally plausible and useful theories co-exist, few people would suggest that either drug use in general or drug dependence are caused by any single factor. It seems that drug use in general is the outcome of interactions between the drug, the personal characteristics of the individual and their environment. It is clear then that drug use stems from many reasons and is the subject of many research interests. It is equally clear that it would be unrealistic to conclude that research in any single field has all the answers.

That said, three general types of theory have been suggested. These are constitutional, individual and environmental.

---

from *Drugs in Perspective* by Martin Plant, Hodder and Stoughton 1987

Constitutional (or biological) approaches

These are concerned with either biological predispositions or with the relationship between a drug and the body.

It has been suggested that depressant drugs such as alcohol, barbiturates and tranquillisers might appeal to those in need of relaxation while stimulants, such as cocaine and amphetamines, might appeal to extroverts who are predisposed to hyperactivity. Animal research has shown that sometimes there does exist a genetic predisposition to use specific drugs. There is a growing body of evidence that inherited factors can predispose some people to develop alcohol-related problems. Such factors obviously interact with availability, social context and other important influences on drug use.

In recent years considerable interest has been aroused by the discovery that the body produces opiate-like substances. It had been known for over 20 years that the human brain has specific receptors for opiates. It now appears that these receptors, in addition to responding to externally produced opiates such as morphine and heroin, respond to a group of internally produced *peptides*. Some of these substances, called endorphins (literally 'the body's own morphine') closely resemble opiates. The receptors excited by such substances are concentrated in the pathways of the brain that are concerned with the perception of pain. In consequence it is an important and intriguing possibility that the development of opiate dependence by some people, or even the general use of certain drugs, may be explained by the ability of some substances to modify the perception of profound experiences such as pleasure and pain.

Individual approaches

Individual approaches are largely concerned with either unusual personality traits (in the case of drug dependent individuals) or far more general factors such as extroversion which may explain willingness to experiment with cannabis or to indulge in other forms of drug use.

Personality characteristics

It is a commonplace belief that drug dependence is at least partly attributable to personality abnormalities, and many studies have supported this conclusion. Even so, the evidence for this view is confusing to say the least, because it is based upon a comparison of 'drugtakers' with 'others'. It does appear that opiate users are probably more neurotic than 'normal' people, but this is not a universal conclusion. And although some institutionalised drugtakers have been noted to exhibit higher than average 'hostility scores', they are not unique in so doing. There are, after all, plenty of neurotic, hostile non-drug users. More generally, it has been noted that if any kind of drug is widely acceptable, as is alcohol, then there is no reason at all why users should have unusual personalities.

Intelligence

Evidence shows that drugtakers are of average or above average intelligence. This conclusion is supported by studies of drugtakers in treatment, educational and penal institutions and in the general population. It is clear that drugtakers vary a great deal in many respects, and there is little support for the view that drug use in caused by lack of intelligence.

General psychiatric state

It is evident that drug dependants in treatment institutions are often psychiatrically disturbed. Sometimes this could result from drug misuse, but there is also evidence that sometimes individuals displayed signs of disturbance before becoming drugtakers. Case history data are often cited to support the view that drugtaking satisfies a variety of psychological needs and that sometimes drug dependence is secondary to a clearly defined psychiatric illness. However, it is possible of course that both psychiatric disturbance and drugtaking may be caused by some other factor. It cannot necessarily be assumed that they invariably lead to one another.

Gender

Men appear far more likely than women to use psychoactive drugs (tranquillisers and depressants excepted) and to be heavy users or dependent upon such substances. There may be many explanations for this. Biological or personality differences between the sexes may predispose men to be drugtakers. Certainly social pressures have traditionally inhibited women even from using legal and socially approved drugs (although these inhibitions are waning – there is evidence to suggest that young women are now more likely to smoke than young men).

Age

Most illegal drug users are young, as are most of those who experience alcohol-related problems. There has been much speculation about whether or not age affects drug dependence. It is probable that youthful anxieties and sexual uncertainties may encourage the use of certain drugs. Also the menopause in women, and old age in general, may often generate pressures that make drug use attractive. On the other hand, if drug use is attributable to personality predispositions, there is no reason why it should be especially prevalent among certain age groups.

Drug use as self-medication

Most drugs have clearly defined effects. It is possible that people who have high anxiety levels or other psychological needs use drugs specifically for this reason, to adjust their 'unsatisfactory' mental state to a more acceptable level. Many drug users certainly report that they use drugs 'to get high', 'to feel relaxed', 'for the experience'. People who are drug dependent also frequently account for their reliance upon drugs in similar terms – 'I use drugs to stop being depressed.'

It is difficult to assess how truthful or perceptive such accounts are. Precise motivation for complex acts are hard to pin down accurately. The main problem is that one cannot guess what would have happened if drugs had not been used. That depression and anxiety are commonplace among drug addicts is not reason enough to conclude that they adopted drug use as a calculated means of countering such conditions.

Hedonism

Drugs can be fun. They offer an accessible and often reliable means of obtaining enjoyable experiences. Anyone who doubts this should remember that most adults use drugs (alcohol, tobacco, coffee) and appear to accept uncritically that such use is valuable. By their own admission, drug users make it abundantly clear that they take drugs in the most part because they like it. By definition, drugs alter the user's mental state – slowing, speeding or distorting perceptions – and many autobiographical accounts of drug use emphasise the appeal of these effects.

A basic human need?

As noted above, psychoactive drug use is virtually universal in some form or other. It has been suggested that this may be so because there is a basic human need to experience an altered state of consciousness. This is compatible with the fact that most people use drugs and most people are clearly not psychologically disturbed. This is really a philosophical theory but it merits consideration in the face of the willingness of such huge numbers of people to use drugs in whatever way and for whatever effect.

Curiosity

Numerous studies of drug use in social settings report that curiosity is often stated to be the reason for initial drug use. This is as true of alcohol and tobacco as it is of cannabis, LSD, solvents, cocaine or opiates. This view, propounded by the drugtakers themselves, may however be partisan. Even if curiosity does account for initial drug use, it does not explain why some users become dependent while others do not.

Self-destruction/risk-taking

The obvious dangers of unwise or excessive drug use have led to speculation that sometimes drugtaking is prompted by self-destructive impulses. Alcohol dependence, for example, has been called 'chronic suicide'. This theory is compatible with the fact that many institutionalised drugtakers appear to have poor self-images and sometimes have quite strong feelings of hostility directed at themselves. It is also consistent with the fact that some drugtakers, for whatever reasons, do overdose on psychoactive substances. Another theory is that drug use is a form of risk-taking. But there is little evidence that drugtakers are particularly predisposed to take risks. Even so, it does appear that some individuals probably choose drugs which produce effects compatible with their personalities or emotional needs.

Resolution of personal problems

Clinical studies indicate that many drug dependent people have serious personal problems. In addition, youthful illegal drug use is often a symbolic gesture of defiance against parental or authority values. It is also possible that adopting the lifestyle of the drugtaker (or the 'regular' at the local) provides some people with friendship and social support. There is little doubt that strong social pressures exist, encouraging individuals to conform to certain patterns of drug use as part of more general lifestyles. As ever though, it is difficult to 'work backwards' and deduce whether an individual's current drug use is attributable to pre-existing poor social relationships.

Environmental approaches

Environmental approaches relate drug use to wider social and cultural factors. Many studies have examined the life experiences of drugtakers, emphasising issues such as broken homes, delinquency, educational and occupational disadvantages. It has also been suggested that social changes or deprivation sometimes precipitate or foster drug use. The following section examines some of these environmental factors.

Family disturbance

Much attention has been focused on the family background of drugtakers, especially of drug dependent individuals in treatment institutions. Many studies of such clinic populations have noted that a high proportion have come from abnormal or disturbed homes and that excessive drug use or drug dependence does sometimes appear to have been aggravated by a family problem of some sort.

The suggested link between drug misuse and parental separation or other family disruptions becomes far less clear-cut when drugtakers are compared to other people. There is no clear evidence that drugtakers *do* differ in this respect from non-drugtakers. In addition, surveys provide abundant evidence that the majority of casual or experimental drug users do not come from disturbed homes.

There is evidence however that many institutionalised drug dependants (including problem drinkers) report having parents who were themselves alcohol or drug misusers or who were otherwise unhappy or disturbed. It is widely noted that institutionalised drug dependants often come from 'loveless homes' or have been 'excessively protected'. A result of this appears to be the limited abilities of some of these individuals to form satisfactory relationships or to communicate with other people. There is little doubt that very often one generation will imitate the drug use of their predecessors. Parents who use drugs excessively may well produce children who do the same, even if they do so with substances of which their parents strongly disapprove, such as cannabis or heroin.

Unemployment, education and work problems

There is abundant and convincing evidence that many institutionalised young drugtakers exhibit signs of educational disturbance, particularly truancy. In addition many 'drop out' of further or higher education or have had very poor employment records. In fact, a growing body of evidence suggests that illegal drug use in the United Kingdom is associated with unemployment. In contrast, tobacco use has clearly declined as unemployment has risen. Young unemployed people appear to be particularly susceptible to illegal drugs, but the relationship between drugs and unemployment is complex and requires further research.

Social class

Drugtaking and drug dependence occur at all social levels. Illegal drug use in America has often been connected with severe social deprivation, for example among poor urban ghetto dwellers. A similar picture has developed in some deprived areas of Britain. Despite this, drug users are drawn from all social classes – in fact, a recent national survey found that the higher socioeconomic groups were the most prominent in drug usage.

The youthfulness of many drugtakers implies that few will have attained their final occupational level. Even so, many surveys have shown that experimental drug use is quite common among students (who are predominantly from non-manual backgrounds). Social class also appears to influence patterns of drug use. It has been suggested that drug users from working class backgrounds are more likely to be heavy or excessive users of a wide range of drugs. Those from middle class families are generally more restrained and selective.

Peer pressure

One of the most commonly given reasons for initial drug use is peer pressure – being goaded into it by friends and acquaintances – and a very large number of studies support this view. This appears to be as applicable to heroin injectors as to cannabis smokers. Some young people appear to be especially likely to be subject to social pressures to indulge in drug use. These include the unemployed, people whose jobs encourage drinking or students and others living away from their parental homes. All are likely to be exposed to, if not influenced by, the fashions and enthusiasms of their peers. Sometimes this pressure will generate strong social endorsement for using cannabis, LSD or heroin.

There is plentiful evidence to support the view that peer pressure is often a potent reason for beginning or continuing drug use. This conclusion rests largely upon self-reporting by drug users who may be reluctant to concede that their use was motivated by any 'abnormal' causes. It is also possible that disturbed or impressionable individuals may be particularly susceptible to peer pressure. This is consistent with the frequently expressed criticism that drug use is sometimes due to 'falling into bad company'. The fact is that from the drug user's point of view the company is often very good. It is clear that people will normally only be influenced by those who they like and wish to be accepted by. There is very little evidence to support the view, beloved of certain tabloid newspapers, that innocent children are lured on to the rocks of addiction by commercially motivated pushers lurking outside the nursery.

Ideology

Some types of drug use are much more widely accepted and indulged in than others. Alcohol and tobacco are generally seen as symbols of maturity and sociability. Medically prescribed tranquillisers and sleeping pills are not seen in this way, and their use is much less discussed or publicly paraded. And finally, illegal drugs carry a whole 'belief system' with them, often regarded as being indicative of protest against or rejection of conventional attitudes and values.

During the 1960s drug use, especially that of cannabis and LSD, was widely linked with the emergence of a distinctive 'teenage culture' associated in the public mind with permissiveness and hedonism. 'Turn on, tune in, drop out' and other slogans clearly linked drugs with the hippy movement and with a variety of 'new' religious cults.

There is a clear relationship between religious ideology and the use of illegal drugs. Self-reports by young drugtakers, especially those deeply involved with drug use, showed that during the 1960s and 1970s most regarded themselves as not sharing their parents' religious views. It could be that the very illegality of drugs frightens off people with conventional and orthodox beliefs. It certainly seems that strong religious views may 'insulate' young people from experimenting with illegal drugs. Religion certainly appears to influence alcohol use and is often a reason why people choose not to drink at all. This applies not only to Islamic countries but also to parts of Scotland and to large areas of the United States.

Delinquency

Many institutionalised drug dependants have criminal records preceding their drug use. This is also true of institutionalised problem drinkers. As noted above, any type of unusual or anti-social behaviour may predispose those indulging in it to break other social conventions. For this reason people who have a criminal history may be more prepared to begin using illegal drugs than would others. In addition some of the factors which foster illegal drug use may be the same as those prompting other types of crime. In spite of this, the overwhelming majority of those using illegal drugs are not otherwise delinquent.

Occupation

Some professions certainly expose people to distinctive social pressures and other stresses. Those in medical, nursing and associated occupations have long been known to be at high risk of becoming drug dependent. Until the 'post-war boom' of youthful heroin use, virtually the only people known to be dependent on opiates in Britain were those in professions which gave them ready access to drugs (usually morphine) or individuals who had become drug dependent while undergoing medical treatment. Doctors have also widely been reported to have high rates of alcohol problems. It is important to remember that the medical profession is relatively well informed about the effects of drugs – calling into question the view that drug problems arise from a lack of knowledge.

Availability

To a large extent, specific drugs are used because they are available. Most social groups use whatever substances they have ready access to. Many young drug users, particularly those in treatment institutions, appear to be willing to use whatever is to hand. Not everyone is so catholic in their drug tastes. Even so it has often been noted that when, for any reason, large amounts of a drug are available at a reasonable price from whatever source, their use and misuse will invariably increase. The extent of alcohol and tobacco use, for instance, is certainly related to their high levels of availability. There is also abundant evidence that the consumption of any drug, be it heroin or alcohol, is influenced by its price relative to other drugs.

Studies of drug users show that whatever their previous characteristics and inclinations, the availability of drugs in conducive surroundings is an important reason for initial use. The upsurge in drug use which began in the 1960s has been attributed in large measure to the introduction of new drug types, either because they had just been 'invented' or because they were being imported from other countries. The fashion for using amphetamines recreationally was certainly encouraged by the vast quantities available either through thefts or through prescription. In addition the upsurge in heroin use in the 1960s and 1970s was clearly exacerbated by casual prescribing so that 'spare' supplies could be passed on to others eager to experiment.

As the above should have hinted, the National Health Service is one of the major suppliers of drugs in Britain. Prescribed drugs have certainly been re-sold, stolen or just left around for others to take. Some of those receiving prescriptions have accidentally become 'therapeutically dependent' upon opiates, barbiturates, tranquillisers and other substances. It is clear that even drugs which are considered to be relatively 'safe', such as Ativan, Librium and Valium, will be misused provided that they are available in sufficient quantities.

The medical profession has frequently tried to deal with this 'leakage'. The famous 'Ipswich Experiment', when doctors voluntarily curtailed amphetamine prescribing, proved beyond doubt that controlling the supply of drugs may sometimes drastically reduce their misuse. Such restrictions will, of course, only work if the demand for such drugs is comparatively low and if no alternative sources of supply exist. The classic western example of an attempt to control the availability of a drug was Prohibition in the United States (1920-33). During this period, while 'conventional' alcohol-related problems such as liver cirrhosis declined dramatically, others emerged in the form of bootlegging and gangsterism. Even in Britain today it is clear that curtailing a wide range of drug use requires considerable Customs, police, court and penal resources. In addition, restricting the legitimate supply of any drug creates the risk that illicit supplies may be sought instead. These may be poorly manufactured, adulterated or impure. Furthermore, infringements on civil liberties and the imposition of harsh penalties may cause more harm than the drugs themselves would otherwise do.

Historical reasons

There has been considerable discussion about why certain types of drug use, especially recreational drug use, blossoms when it does. Very often the explanations are clear cut – the introduction of tobacco to Britain by Sir Walter Raleigh or the production of new drugs by the pharmaceutical industry. More often than not though, explanations are hard to pin down – the emergence of a distinctive youth drug culture during the 1950s and 1960s occurred for a myriad of reasons, many of which remain only partly understood.

It has been noted that even during the 1940s and earlier, a certain amount of drug trafficking was carried out by sailors. Cannabis use also received a boost from American musicians and 'beat' poets. Even so, there is little to suggest that either of these influences went much beyond the dockyard gates or the fringes of the avant-garde. The arrival of West Indian immigrants to Britain during the 1950s certainly introduced for the first time fairly large numbers of people used to smoking cannabis. Some of these immigrants certainly continued their cannabis smoking, but it is difficult to see them actively influencing the host community. That said, while immigrant cannabis use was probably fairly self-contained, it may have contributed to the general spread of the recreational use of 'new' drugs. It is also probable that, like many other fashions from wearing jeans to break dancing, certain types of drug use were adopted due to American influence.

The whole lifestyle of young adults changed during the 1960s. Pop music, 'permissiveness' and 'hippy culture' arrived, and drugs were legitimised by cult figures and the new generation of millionaire rock superstars in the 1970s. Youth culture was established with a heavy emphasis on rebellion against established norms. Invariably the drugs used complemented the musical preferences of the user, which was often explicitly drug-oriented. Amphetamines fuelled the Northern soul circuit, helping dancers stay awake all night, while cannabis soothed the strains of softer sounds and LSD helped the listener appreciate Pink Floyd. With the demise of the hippy, came the nihilism of punk with its glue and heroin. More recently, dance has made a comeback, with the rave introducing a raft of new 'feel good' drugs such as ecstasy.

Many people (politicians and newspaper editors among them) make the simplistic assumption that drug use is caused by the activities of traffickers and dealers. In fact, most studies conclude that initial drug use is largely attributable to encouragement by friends. The direct influence of commercially motivated suppliers has almost certainly been over-emphasised. In more general terms there is a great deal of evidence supporting the view that young people's drug use largely spreads in a friendly and hospitable way, reflecting much wider social changes. That said, drug use is fostered both by demand and supply and – as noted by Freemantle (1985) – the international drug trade is a massive and relentlessly expanding industry.

The increase in officially recorded drug dependence may be a logical corollary of the growing acceptance of all forms of drug use. Because relatively large numbers of people were prepared to experiment with substances such as cannabis and LSD in the 1960s, a minority may have been encouraged to use opiates. Even so, such a conclusion is by no means certain and the great majority of illegal drug users appear to confine themselves to casual experimentation.

Sociological theories

Several sociological theories have been applied to the post-war spread of drugs in Britain. Probably the most important views are that drug use reflects an increase in *alienation* or *anomie*. Such theories attribute drug use to new social pressures, such as competition for jobs, housing and education. Those whose needs are left unmet by the mainstream of society simply opt out, turning instead to the supportive 'alternative' lifestyle of the drug scene. This provides status and companionship without the demands of the mundane, workaday world. Instead of having to accept the constraints of 'straight' society, with its long-term planning and deferment of gratification, the drug scene permits instant enjoyment. Because of its free and easy values, the scene allows people to 'do their own thing' and becomes a haven for individuals who, for whatever reasons, cannot or will not fit into the rat race of the broader society. This view certainly makes some sense of the commitment to drugtaking. It is also consistent with the fact that many drug dependent people have psychological problems or are socially deprived. In particular this approach has the merit of linking drug use with the structure of society.

Another sociological view is that once a 'deviant' behaviour, such as drugtaking, becomes evident society attempts to control it and inadvertently makes it worse. The logic of this theory is that as drugtaking is labelled and legislated against, those who indulge in it become more secretive and more cut off – their deviance is 'amplified'. Consequently, the social controls against this 'growing' problem are increased which, in turn, ratchets the deviants into further isolation and so on. This theory provides a useful insight into the possible effects of identifying and attempting to curb a newly defined social problem. There is much truth in this view and some drugtakers certainly appear to enjoy the drama conferred upon their activities by legislation and by their battles against those who enforce it.

As this chapter has attempted to show, many plausible theories have been put forward to explain why people use drugs and why some become dependent upon them. Each of these theories is consistent with the characteristics of some drugtakers, but it is clear that no single theory can account for all types of drug use. Drugtaking and drug dependence appear to be influenced by a great number of factors, whether constitutional, individual or environmental. Probably different reasons account for different types of drug use. The casual or experimental use of drugs is probably due largely to social pressures combined with availability. Dependence upon drugs may well be attributable to much more profound factors such as social deprivation or psychological disturbance. And finally, other factors may account for the way some people remain dependent while others do not.

How many drug users are there?

by Oswin Baker & John Marsden

In spite of the level of concern which surrounds drug misuse, we have a far from adequate picture of the extent and patterning of illicit use in Britain at the national level. Population statistics are readily to hand for alcohol, tobacco and prescribed medicines. However, no regular, reliable national surveys record drug misuse in the way that, say, the nation's drinking and smoking are monitored by the General Household Survey. With no 'official' national drugs survey one of the most basic questions about drug misuse – how much of it is there? – is left unanswered.

One of the worst consequences of this blind spot is that it leaves the field open to wishful thinking, anecdotal assertions, propaganda, rumour, exaggeration, and potentially wildly inaccurate guesswork. Nevertheless, bearing the above caveats in mind, the few pieces of information that we do have – several large-scale surveys and numerous regional studies – do allow us to draw a highly valid picture.

Prevalence

Cannabis is undoubtedly the most widely misused drug in the UK. It is consistently found that the great majority of people who have ever used any illegal drug have used cannabis. This means that the extent of cannabis use can be taken as a rough guide to the overall extent of illegal drug use in Britain.

In 1989, MORI surveyed a representative sample of British adults. 1,079 people aged 18 and over were interviewed, and it was found that five per cent admitted to having used cannabis (seven per cent of the men and three per cent of the women).

In previous editions of *Drug Misuse in Britain* we have also quoted the 1982 British Crime Survey (BCS), which reinforced the five per cent ballpark figure for cannabis use. The 1992 Survey, however, casts doubt on this rather low estimate for

---

Extract from Baker O., Marsden J. *Drug misuse in Britain 1994*. ISDD, 1995.
Available from ISDD

the use of the drug. Over 10,000 people in England and Wales aged 12 to 59 were interviewed about their experience of and attitudes towards crime, and three-quarters of them completed an anonymous questionnaire about drug and solvent misuse. Fourteen per cent of this sample admitted to having ever used cannabis.

While the most obvious explanation for this rise is a rise in drug use itself, the three-fold increase could be explained away by the exclusion of Scotland from these figures or the inclusion of 12-15 year olds in the sample. It is highly unlikely however that Scotland would pull down the proportion of drug misusers or that a few 'bragging adolescents' would have such a marked effect. It has to be accepted that both the 1982 BCS and (given its similar results and methodology) the MORI survey may have underestimated the extent of cannabis use and therefore of illegal drug use in general. Specifically, both depended on admissions of criminal activity made in a face-to-face interview. Using a revised interview schedule to improve willingness to admit criminalactivity, the 1984 British Crime Survey already found that 2.9 per cent of its sample of those aged 16 and over in England and Wales admitted to using cannabis *in the past year* – 70 per cent more than the corresponding figure in the 1982 survey.

As for the 1992 survey, its estimate of recent use (as opposed to lifetime use) is nearly triple that of the 1982 survey. Five per cent of the total sample (two per cent a decade earlier) said they'd used cannabis the previous year, about a third of those who had ever used the drug.

1992 was a good year for large-scale studies. A general population survey of 5000 people aged 16 and over in four urban centres was also carried out by researchers from Sheffield University, funded by the Central Drugs Prevention Unit (CDPU). Not only did each location provide a general sample of 1000 people, but also a 'booster' group of 250 young people thought to be most 'at risk' from drug use. When the figures for lifetime use of cannabis are averaged out, it appears that 15 per cent of the main sample had used the drug, confirming the view of the 1992 BCS that one in seven of the general population has used cannabis. When recent use is studied, it was found that seven per cent of the main sample had taken the drug in the last year, again broadly in line with the BCS findings.

The history of the BCS highlights the difficulty in making hard and fast assertions about the population's drug use based solely on the returns from household surveys. But when the 1992 survey is placed alongside the CDPU figures, a substantial re-evaluation of the benchmark for drug misuse in Britain is urgently demanded. Seventeen per cent of the BCS and 18 per cent of the CDPU samples admitted to lifetime use of any drug, suggesting that a bottomline figure of one in six people will have used illegal drugs at some time in their life. Using these estimates leads to the conclusion that in any one year at least six per cent of the population (double the proportion in 1982) will take a drug illicitly – some three million people.

Although estimates of drug use from population surveys are illuminating, they may be misleading if applied to different sub-populations. For example, the 1992 BCS found that three men to every two women admitted lifetime drug use, while the 1989 MORI survey found that two men to every woman admitted cannabis use. Whenever Britain's drug use is talked about, while it should be recognised that the majority of users are male, it must also be remembered that between a quarter and a third are female.

Young people

As well as gender, age is a major factor. Most surveys concur that during the years of compulsory schooling, illegal drug use is considerably less common than in the young adult years. Very low rates of drug trial at age 13-14 peak by age 19-20 to the levels described in the following section. Again, the 1992 BCS can give us a ballpark figure for under-16 use: three per cent of the 12 and 13 year olds questioned claimed to have taken drugs (one per cent for cannabis), while 14 per cent of 14 and 15 year olds reported drug use (nine per cent for cannabis).

No survey, however, has provided the definitive answer to the sensitive issue of the extent of school age drug use. Some have small samples, some large but not representative of the UK school population, and all may have suffered from the probability that drug users were less likely than non-users to be at home or in school when the survey was done. Several caution that young people's statements regarding their drug use can be unreliable: one survey, for instance, found claims of heroin use among 13-year-old boys to be hitting five per cent compared with the perhaps more believable claim of two per cent among 16-year-olds.

The largest samples in 1993, 29,074 pupils aged 11-16 from 171 schools are achieved in John Balding's annual survey for Exeter University's Schools Health Education Unit. Samples are not selected on a random or representative basis but depend largely on the goodwill of district health authorities. Since 1987, the surveys have included questions on drug use amongst the participating pupils.

Balding argues that his survey results have been shown to be close to those found by representative surveys (most notably the MORI/HEA survey detailed below), and that the studies' validity is likely to be high as schools have an interest in encouraging accurate responses. A large sample and the availability of data collected in the same way from previous years make this a uniquely useful source but one that cannot be assumed to fully reflect the national picture as the results have often been regionally weighted. (Balding himself has described a so-called 'Yorkshire effect' in the figures for 1991, when schools from that county tilted the balance of responses.)

In 1993, three per cent of Year 7 pupils (aged 11-12) reported taking illegal drugs or solvents, rising to six per cent in Year 8 (aged 12-13), 15 per cent in Year 9, 23 per cent in Year 10, and 31 per cent in Year 11. At least 15 per cent of 13-16 year olds recorded trying cannabis, while 28 per cent of Year 11 boys and 22 per cent of Year 11 girls admitted using cannabis leaf.

The next largest sample was achieved by MORI in a survey conducted in October to November 1989 for the HEA. 10,293 9-15 year old school pupils in England drawn from a nationally representative sample of 551 state and independent schools were questioned. Ninety-four per cent of pupils in the participating schools completed the questionnaire: seven per cent of the total sample had tried drugs or solvents and four per cent took cannabis.

Among 9-12-year olds, experimentation with any drug except solvents was at one per cent or less, but by 15, 16 per cent of boys and 14 per cent of girls claimed to have tried cannabis. Although so much of the information on school children must be handled with care, this cannabis data, at least, is very similar to Balding's. In his 1993 survey, 15 per cent and 14 per cent of 15 year old boys and girls had tried the drug.

In April 1989 the company RBL conducted the latest in a series of surveys begun in 1985 to evaluate government anti-drug campaigns. These each sampled about 720 people aged 13-20 across England and Wales and the results were weighted to be representative of the general population of this age. Lower use rates in the school-age group were reported in most of the stages of the evaluation. In 1989, only four per cent of 15-16 year olds reported ever having used cannabis. In previous years back to 1985 this figure was six or seven per cent. These relatively low rates of reported drug use could however be ascribed to the fact that the RBL surveys were the only household ones (all the others being carried out in the school) and the results could therefore have been influenced significantly by the presence of parents in the home.

Scotland, Wales and Northern Ireland each have a fair number of recent – and reasonably representative – surveys of school-age drug use.

In 1988, a study was carried out in Scotland as part of a national evaluation of drug education. Although its sample was not intended to be nationally representative, it did embrace nearly 1200 13-16 year old pupils from 20 urban schools in the Edinburgh, Glasgow and Dundee areas, each school supplying a mixed sex and mixed ability group typical of that school. Overall, 11 per cent of pupils aged 13-14 had tried illegal drugs (excluding solvents) rising to 22 per cent at age 14-15, and 27 per cent at age 15-16. Four years later, Grampian Health Board surveyed 10 per cent of 13-17 year-old pupils in its region – 27 per cent had taken an illegal drug.

In Wales, three surveys have recently been carried out, which were also not intended to be nationally representative but by dint of their size can be broadly treated as being so. In 1989, Gwynedd Health Authority carried out a survey of the Fourth Year pupils in all of the county's secondary schools. The 2,467 respondents represented over 80 per cent of the county's Fourth Year pupils, and the same proportion were 15 years old. Seven per cent had taken illegal drugs and five per cent had tried cannabis.

The second Welsh study was carried out in Mid-Glamorgan in 1990. All 13-18 year olds in three-quarters of the county's comprehensive schools were surveyed, and 13,437 responded. Nine per cent admitted to taking illicit drugs, eight per cent reporting cannabis use. Overall, 23 per cent of the group, of whom the majority (52 per cent) were girls, had taken some substance illicitly.

Finally, in 1990 a random sample of secondary school pupils were surveyed in Wales, which included 2,239 15-16 year olds. Twenty-one per cent of this age group claimed to have used drugs or solvents, half of whom had used them in the last month. In a 1992 follow-up, 37 per cent of Fifth Formers reported drug use, 80 per cent of whom had tried cannabis.

As for Northern Ireland, in 1992 the Southern Health and Social Services Board (covering nearly a quarter of the province's land mass) surveyed five per cent of 14-19 year-olds in the region. Over half had been offered drugs, and a third had tried them. Two-fifths of these admitted to regular use.

In summary, somewhere between a seventh and a third of schoolchildren in Britain are likely to have tried drugs.

Young adults

The years between the end of compulsory schooling at 16 and the approach of middle age at around 35 years are consistently found to be the peak period for illegal drug use.

In the 1992 British Crime Survey, active use of cannabis was practically limited to the under-30s. Twenty-four per cent of respondents aged 16-29 said they had experienced lifetime use of cannabis, while 18 per cent of respondents aged 16-19 and 14 per cent of 20-24 year olds said they had used the drug in 1991. The corresponding recent use figure for those in their 30s was more like three per cent and for those over 40, under two per cent. As for those who'd ever taken any drug, 28 per cent of 16-29s admitted to doing so while 14 per cent of them had taken at least one illicit drug the previous year.

MORI's survey found that 12 per cent of 18-24 year olds had smoked cannabis. In the lower part of this age range 15 per cent of 18-21 year olds said they had done so. Admission of cannabis smoking fell to four per cent among 35-54 year olds and to one per cent among those aged 55 and over.

The results of the CDPU survey show higher rates of lifetime and recent use of any drug among young people. Thirty-six per cent of the main sample's 16-19 year olds, and 41 per cent of its 20-24 year olds had taken drugs at some time, while 26 per cent and 21 per cent respectively had taken a drug in the last year.

It is among young men that experience of cannabis (and drug use in general) is most prevalent. In the MORI survey 14 per cent of 18-34 year old men had tried cannabis. In the 1992 BCS, a third of men between 16 and 29 said they had tried a drug in the past, while 28 per cent of 16 to 19 year old men reported using drugs in the previous year. The survey's corresponding proportions for women are 23 per cent and 15 per cent, and of those admitting to lifetime drug use, 40 per cent of over 16s were female.

Considering that about 85 per cent of young adults admitting to drug use in both the CDPU study and the BCS would have taken cannabis, from all the above general population surveys it can be conservatively estimated that one in three young men and one in five young women have tried cannabis. This would imply a both-sex average of, say, a minimum of 25 per cent for cannabis use.

Several surveys which have concentrated on the young adult age band confirm that these rough estimates lie at the lower end of probability.

The CDPU survey can provide us with more targeted information on young people. Its 'booster' sample of 1000 people between the ages of 16 and 29 also took account of the nature of 'risk', being aimed those of low socio-economic status living in deprived inner-city areas. In this group, 42 per cent of 16-19 year olds had taken drugs at some time while 44 per cent of 20-24 year olds had done so. Between 20 and 30 per cent of 16-29 year olds had used a drug in the last year.

If the booster sample's figures are transposed on the national scale, then one in four of those in 'high risk' groups have used a drug recently, one in three have taken cannabis at some time, and as many as one in two will have lifetime use of drugs.

A Gallup survey conducted in spring 1989 for the Miller Lite lager company found that perhaps a third of young men have tried drugs. Thirty-one per cent of a representative sample of 1500 18-35 year old men in Britain disagreed (or disagreed strongly) with the proposition that they had "never tried using any drug except on prescription". A third of 18-21 year old men disagreed, implicitly admitting to drug misuse of some sort. Only among 30-35 year olds did admission of drug misuse fall below 30 per cent, to 25 per cent.

The figures from the 1989 RBL survey for 19 and 20 year olds seem to be more reliable than for the younger age groups. Twenty-nine per cent of the 177 19-20 year-olds sampled had tried cannabis.

In March to May 1990 a household interview survey conducted by MORI for the Health Education Authority (HEA) sampled 4436 16-19 year olds in England who were available for interview out of a nationally representative random sample of 7711. Eighteen per cent of the sample refused to say which drugs they had tried. Of the rest (3655, less than half the original random sample), 32 per cent had tried drugs including 37 per cent of men and 26 per cent of women; 25 per cent of the 16-19 year olds claim to have tried cannabis.

Drug trial rates increased for men from 29 per cent at age 16 to 49 per cent at age 19 and for women from 18 per cent to 33 per cent, meaning that before their twentieth birthday 41 per cent of the sample had misused drugs or solvents. At age 19, 41 per cent of men and 25 per cent of women claim to have tried cannabis (a third of the sample).

Besides the 1992 BCS and the CDPU study, the most recent national survey was conducted by Gallup for Wrangler in 1992 and sampled 625 15-24 year olds in Britain. Of these, 29 per cent had tried illegal drugs or solvents and 23 per cent had taken cannabis.

There is a large measure of agreement between this survey, the BCS and the CDPU and HEA household surveys, the only ones to have sampled during the '90s. Each found that about a third of young adults had tried drugs or solvents and a quarter cannabis.

All the surveys reviewed so far systematically sampled to achieve a set of respondents representative of the general population. In 1988, by way of contrast, a Gallup survey covering England and Wales sampled nearly 1900 university and polytechnic students aged 18 upwards. The question put to them was whether they had used drugs since becoming a student, so the results are not comparable to studies cited above which asked respondents if they had ever used a drug.

Around one in five of the 18-21 year old students said they had taken cannabis. Reported drug use rates were higher among older (22-30 years of age) students, but, except for cannabis (27 per cent), none of the figures for other drugs exceeded six per cent.

In 1993, a Europe-wide survey was carried out amongst 4260 students. Thirty-seven per cent of the British sample had taken drugs (compared to the European average of 29 per cent) and 28 per cent of British students claimed to take drugs regularly.

Another example of a non-representative survey is provided by the London entertainment magazine, Time Out, which in 1993 questioned 262 twenty-five year-old readers about their lifestyles. Although the sample is quite small and locally/socially-circumscribed, the survey can still provide a rough and ready snapshot of young adult life in the capital. Three-quarters of respondents reported having taken drugs, of whom 97 per cent had used cannabis, 40 per cent amphetamines, 38 per cent ecstasy, 33 per cent LSD and 32 per cent cocaine. In 1994 a similar survey was carried out although it appears to be based much more readily on a drug-using population. Questionnaires were returned by 903 readers, of whom three-quarters were between the ages of 19 and 34. Eighty-seven per cent had experimented with drugs, 99 per cent of whom claimed to have used cannabis; 61 per cent had tried amphetamines, 56 per cent LSD, 52 per cent cocaine and 47 per cent ecstasy. While these studies may not provide too reliable a gauge of general drug use, they do give a clear picture of the preferred drugs of choice amongst urban recreational drug users.

Summary of findings on prevalence

The available national surveys together suggest that around a quarter to a third of young people have tried solvents or illegal drugs by their twentieth birthday. Around a third of young men and one in five young women will have done so. The great majority of these – perhaps a quarter of the young adult population – have tried cannabis. Estimates are more risky for other drugs as there is less information and smaller use rates render findings more liable to sampling variation.

Above 35 years of age drug misuse is considerably less common and the same applies to the years before the end of compulsory schooling. Britain still has a generally drug-free school-age population, but one in which contact with drugs other than cannabis and solvents is no longer uncommon. Heroin or cocaine use among school pupils remains a rarity. The studies cited so far permit some informed estimates of the order of magnitude of this contact, but estimates are what they remain, a rule of thumb seriously lacking a verifiable set of data.

By 15-16 years of age, probably a fifth and maybe a quarter of young people have ever tried solvents or illegal drugs, though regular use is confined to perhaps two per cent for cannabis and below one per cent for other drugs. At age 13-14 perhaps one in 10 children have experience of any illegal drug or solvents.

Perhaps 17 per cent or nearly one in six of young school-leavers have tried cannabis; however in certain schools in certain localities, rates of use may be much higher, as Exeter University's report for 1987 confirmed. In one local area, rates of ever having been offered cannabis varied from over 30 per cent in one school to less than seven per cent in another among children of the same age and sex.

Similarly, the Scottish drug education evaluation study reported lifetime rates of illegal drug use ranging from 57 per cent in one school to eight per cent in another.

However, perhaps the most telling recent surveys were carried out in the North West of England by the University of Manchester. Granted, they were local rather than national studies, but their interest lies in the fact that they surveyed a group of teenagers over a three year period (1991-1993). More than 1000 14-17 year olds finally took part, and the results of the first year largely fit in with other studies – a third of those sampled had used drugs. But by the final year, this proportion had mushroomed: 51 per cent – *the majority* – said they had taken drugs. The final report, *Drugs Futures*, concluded: "Over the next few years, and certainly in urban areas, non-drug trying adolescents will be a minority group. *In one sense they will be the deviants*." Such a situation can only have far-reaching implications for how the issue of drugs is dealt with both on the level of national policy and on the more local level, in Britain's schools.

Drug types

This brings us on to the drug types used. So far only cannabis has been looked at in detail, largely because it is the most used drug and therefore provides a rough and ready estimate of drug use in general. In summary, it can be said with reasonable confidence that at least seven million people between the ages of 12 and 59 have taken cannabis at some time in their lives. Perhaps a quarter of a million schoolchildren and two million young adults will have taken the drug.

Hallucinogens and stimulants

Amongst those who had tried a drug, the recent surveys suggest a trend for more young people to go beyond cannabis to sample amphetamine, LSD and ecstasy. Certainly, amphetamines and hallucinogens (and also amyl nitrite) came out as the next most popular drugs after cannabis in the CDPU study's main sample (with ecstasy joining the throng in the booster). In line with the Wrangler study which showed 10 per cent of young people trying LSD and seven per cent ecstasy, the 1992 BCS showed 11 per cent of 16-19 year olds trying amphetamines, nine per cent ecstasy, and eight per cent LSD. The CDPU confirms these rough figures, with about 10 per cent of the booster having tried magic mushrooms, amphetamines or LSD, and eight per cent ecstasy.

In the 1988 Scottish survey seven per cent of 13-16 year olds had tried magic mushrooms, six per cent LSD and four per cent amphetamines. In 1989 in England the MORI/HEA survey found that by 15, five per cent of boys and two per cent of girls claimed to have tried LSD, four per cent and two per cent respectively had tried amphetamines and three per cent and one per cent ecstasy. The 1990 HEA survey of 16-19s found that amyl nitrite was the next most popular drug after cannabis (10 per cent), followed by seven per cent taking magic mushrooms, six per cent LSD, five per cent amphetamines and three per cent ecstasy. At 19, amyl nitrite had been used by 16 per cent of males and nine per cent of females, magic mushrooms by 14 per cent and eight per cent, amphetamines by 10 per cent and eight per cent, LSD 11 per cent and four per cent, and ecstasy five per cent and one per cent.

As for the 1989 RBL study, 12 per cent of 19 and 20 year olds claimed to have taken magic mushrooms, 10 per cent amphetamines and seven per cent LSD. These higher rates of use are confirmed by more recent studies. In Mid-Glamorgan, 11 per cent were found to have taken magic mushrooms while the 1992 follow-up to the 1990 study records that 18 per cent of Welsh Fifth Formers have tried magic mushrooms, nine per cent LSD, eight per cent amphetamines and five per cent ecstasy.

The Exeter team's 1993 survey showed 15-16 year olds' experimentation with LSD running at 11 per cent (exceeding the use of natural hallucinogens), with amphetamines at 10 per cent, and ecstasy at four per cent. Likewise, the Northern Ireland survey found that 12 per cent had taken LSD, 10 per cent amphetamines, and six per cent ecstasy.

As the last surveys make clear, many of the earlier studies fail to pick up on the rise in the use of ecstasy. In fact, it becomes quickly apparent that research carried out before 1990 on young people's drug usage misses out on the dance drug boom which kicked into gear in 1989, and should therefore be treated with caution when trying to interpret recent trends.

One final word on trends. The CDPU survey explored the associations between drug types. Certain drugs were found to be 'mutually used'. Chief amongst these were LSD, amphetamines and ecstasy: when one of these is taken, the user is likely to take one or both of the others.

When 'non-opiates' were studied (essentially hallucinogens and stimulants), it was found that 72 per cent of the main sample's non-opiate users took cannabis, while only 36 per cent of cannabis users took non-opiates. In other words, while it is usual for non-opiate users to take cannabis, the majority of cannabis users don't take non-opiates.

It was also found that 56 per cent of users of opiates (including cocaine) took non-opiates, yet only 11 per cent of non-opiate users took opiates. This means that while the majority of opiate users take non-opiates, only a minority of non-opiate users take opiates.

Solvents

Solvent use is almost exclusively the preserve of young schoolchildren, but it still feeds into the figures of lifetime use, as demonstrated by the 1992 Wrangler survey of 15-24 year olds. This found that nearly 10 per cent had tried 'sniffing'.

MORI's 1989 survey for the HEA found that in the age range 12-14, three per cent of boys and one to two per cent of girls had tried solvents. At 15 years of age, four per cent of boys and two per cent of girls admitted to solvent use, and three per cent of 16-19 year olds had tried them. These are relatively low experimentation rates compared to several other studies.

In 1988 in Scotland 12 per cent of 13-16 year olds admitted ever having sniffed solvents (but only one in 18 of these used it regularly), the same figure as the Mid-Glamorgan study. Fifteen per cent of those surveyed in Northern Ireland admitted to using solvents at some time.

Exeter University's national report for 1992 showed that more girls than boys admitted sniffing and that experience of solvents rises from less than three per cent among 12-13 year olds to over seven per cent among 14-15 year olds. However, the 1993 study shows a dramatic shift in solvent use: under four per cent of 13-14 year olds and six per cent of 15-16 year olds admitted to having used solvents. Solvents were also no longer used by a higher proportion of girls than boys.

Once again the English anti-drug evaluation study reports lower use rates among school-age respondents relative to other studies, finding that nought to one per cent of secondary school pupils had ever tried solvents.

Cocaine and heroin

The 1989 MORI poll quoted at the beginning of this chapter also asked its sample whether they had "taken hard drugs such as cocaine or heroin". Just one per cent answered yes (two per cent of the men and one per cent of the women). At this level of use the numbers involved were very small – just 12 people altogether, eight men and four women. The 1992 Wrangler study put 'hard drug' use at one per cent too.

This minimal level of use is reflected in all the other surveys, but minimal use does not imply minimal concern – one per cent of 20 to 50 year olds is still a quarter of a million people. Moreover, the 1992 BCS found that although less than one per cent said they had ever taken heroin, four per cent of 25-29 year olds claimed to have taken cocaine.

The CDPU found that heroin, cocaine and crack had been used by one per cent or less of the main sample. However, the main sample also used ecstasy at a similar level. As for the booster of young people 'at risk', crack was still used by one per cent, but heroin and cocaine use had risen to two per cent and four per cent respectively. When associations between drug types were looked at, 96 per cent of the main sample's opiate users also took cannabis and 56 per cent non-opiates (while only seven per cent of cannabis users took opiates and 11 per cent of non-opiate users did so). Opiate users were, therefore, much more likely to take other drugs than other-drug users were to take opiates.

Looking at the school-age population, RBL's 1989 survey, the MORI/HEA schools survey, the 1993 Exeter University questionnaire, and the Scottish, Welsh and Irish studies all found minimal heroin use amongst under-16s, typically between 0.5 and one per cent.

The same studies found experience of cocaine in the same age groups to range from nought to 1.6 per cent.

Confirmation of this order of magnitude of prevalence of cocaine and heroin use can be found in the HEA's 1990 survey of 16-19 year olds in England. Among this age group use of these drugs is likely to be greater than among the school-age population, but even here heroin, cocaine and crack had each been tried by one per cent or less of the sample. The RBL figures for 19 and 20 year olds show a markedly higher level of cocaine use (three per cent) but this is not borne out by any of the other teenage studies.

Demographics and patterns of use

Most surveys confine themselves to measuring the number of people who admit to using a drug at least once, bracketing the one-off user with the addict and all stages in between. Important distinctions are lost in the process. For example, an experimental toke of cannabis may be considered a normal part of growing up but daily use will usually be a cause for concern.

Methods of use can be as significant as what is used and how often. HIV has magnified existing concern over the danger of injecting drugs and also the likelihood of unprotected sex while taking one of the recreational 'love/dance drugs'. There is also evidence that smoking cocaine (in the form of crack) as opposed to sniffing it is more likely to be associated with dependent patterns of use.

The CDPU study contains a large amount of demographic data on patterns of use. Some of this has already been presented here (the associations between the use of drug types), which demonstrates a growing eclecticism of use from cannabis users, through non-opiate users, and finally to opiate users.

There is also a general pattern in frequency of use (cannabis, amphetamines and ecstasy being used most often). Within the main sample, opiate users starkly display either control or addiction, taking their drug daily (six per cent) or hardly at all, but any such polarities are not reflected in the 'booster' sample, which introduces the question as to whether patterns of use are especially problematic.

Lifetime polydrug use was much more pronounced among the 'booster' sample of people at risk, with only 39 per cent of the booster's users sticking to one drug (the proportions were reversed for the main sample, with 57 per cent of users taking only one drug type).

Demographically, the survey found that the most likely user would be a young, white male in the AB or C1 socio-economic groups. ABs from the main sample were twice as likely to have lifetime or recent use of drugs than C2s, and over half of white respondents in one location's booster group had taken drugs while only a third of black respondents had. This would seem to fly in the face of many assumptions about drug users, especially as the other socio-economic variables should have predisposed ethnic minority groups, for example, towards drug use (most were young, male and unemployed). The research poses the question: could much of previous research have been unable to recruit enough of an ethnic mix to test the view that 'black people take drugs'?

Summary of findings on drug types

In the 1990s the most remarkable departure from earlier decades is the integration of LSD and ecstasy into mass youth culture. The other so-called 'dance drug', amphetamine, has a record in youth/dance culture going back to the '60s. Although the rise of LSD and ecstasy may be the highlights, there appears to have been a trend towards greater variety in youth drug use, with the emphasis on stimulants and hallucinogenics but cannabis also being used in a wider variety of situations.

In general, the gaggle of hallucinogenic and stimulant drugs which follow on the heels of cannabis use appear to have been tried by perhaps one in 10 young people, amphetamines and 'magic mushrooms' leading the way, with solvents, LSD and ecstasy each being used by five to 10 per cent of young adults. Tranquilliser misuse may approach 10 per cent in Scotland but across England affects perhaps less than three per cent.

Use of the drugs that most concern the British press and public, heroin and cocaine, is recorded at very low but measurable levels among the young adult population, usually at one per cent or less. Less than one per cent even of young adults, the most 'at risk' group, have ever injected.

Three surveys allow us to track the development of the hallucinogens and stimulants. Most useful is the 1992 Gallup/Wrangler survey of 15-24 year olds which replicated one done in 1989, spanning the rise of a new youth culture centred on rave and dance music. Over those three years admissions of drug use had virtually doubled (from 15 to 29 per cent), ecstasy had risen from obscurity to relative popularity (less than one per cent to seven per cent) and LSD from the experience of only a small minority to a drug tried by one in 10 young adults (up from 2.4 per cent to 10 per cent).

The survey of drug use among 15 year olds in Wales was carried out in 1990 and updated in 1992. In the interim, reported cannabis use all but doubled (16 per cent to 30 per cent), while magic mushroom use rose from 10 per cent to 18 per cent, amphetamines from four per cent to eight per cent, and LSD from three per cent to nine per cent. By 1992, five per cent had taken ecstasy.

Less secure are the trends revealed by John Balding's annual reports based on a health behaviour questionnaire, as the samples are neither nationally representative nor necessarily comparable year on year. A trend to use of dance drugs should be most clearly revealed by comparing results for 15-16 year olds in 1988 with those in 1991 and 1993.

This comparison shows lifetime use of LSD up from less than one per cent to six per cent to 11 per cent, amphetamine up from one per cent to five per cent to 10 per cent, ecstasy listed as a separate drug for the first time in 1991 at four per cent staying level and (despite its expense) entrenching itself in 1993, and cannabis up from four per cent to 11 per cent to 25 per cent.

It could be that this apparent rise in drug use is due to the 1991 and 1993 samples with very high turn-outs from Yorkshire and Scottish schools respectively being drawn from a different pool of young people characterised by higher rates of drug experimentation. It is therefore worth stepping down a year to the 14-15 year olds, where it appears that the 1993 sample (9,676 children) was more nationally representative and perhaps more comparable with the 1988 sample (11,734 children).

At this age lifetime use of LSD, amphetamine and magic mushrooms had each risen from around or below one per cent to five to seven per cent, and cannabis use from two per cent to 16 per cent. In 1993 three per cent of the 14-15 year olds said they had tried ecstasy. Trial of solvents had risen from 3 to five per cent (although this was down on the 1991 figure of six per cent). Results from this age group add weight to the impression of increased and more varied drug use gained from the 15-16 year old samples.

There were few signs of these developments when in April 1989 researchers evaluating government anti-drug campaigns conducted the latest in their series of studies. In 1989 use of any drug, of cannabis, amphetamines or LSD for the age range 13-20 were at unremarkable levels compared to the surveys conducted over the previous four years.

Putting these fragments of evidence together suggests the relatively stable youth drug use patterns of the mid-80s were disturbed in the late '80s and that by the '90s there was increased use of established drugs like cannabis, solvents, amphetamines, and magic mushrooms and an upsurge in use of ecstasy and LSD. As stressed earlier, if this is the case then pre-1990 surveys of young people must be considered suspect as guides to current drug use prevalence and patterns.

Main studies cited in this chapter:

Balding J. *Young people in 1993.* Schools Health Education Unit, University of Exeter, 1994.

Coggans N. *et al. National evaluation of drug education in Scotland.* ISDD, 1991.

Crime, alcohol, drugs and leisure: a survey of 13,437 young people in Mid-Glamorgan. Mid-Glamorgan Social Crime Prevention Unit, 1992.

Gallup. *Miller Lite survey among young people.* Unpublished, 1989.

Gallup/Wrangler. *The youth report.* 1992.

Gallup. *Student survey.* Unpublished, 1989.

Health Education Authority. *Tomorrow's young adults.* HEA, 1992.

Health Education Authority. *Today's young adults.* HEA, 1992.

Illicit drug and solvent use. Southern Health and Social Services Board, Northern Ireland, 1993.

Leitner M. *et al. Drug usage and drugs prevention: the views and habits of the general public.* London Home Office Drugs Prevention Initiative, 1993.

MORI/News of the World. *Modern living.* 1989.

Mott J., Mirrlees-Black C. *Self-reported drug misuse in England and Wales: main findings from the 1992 British Crime Survey.* London Home Office Research and Statistics Department, 1993.

Parker H. *et al. Drugs futures.* ISDD, 1995.

Publicis/AIESEC/IPSOS. *Generation 1993: a study of the views and opinions of European students.* 1993.

RBL. *Anti-heroin campaign evaluation. Report of findings of stages 1-111.* June 1986.

RBL. *Anti-misuse of drugs campaign evaluation: report of findings 1-V11.* July 1989.

Roberts G. *Lifestyle and drugs survey.* Gwynedd Health Authority, 1991.

Smith C. *et al. Youth Life Wales Briefing Paper No 1: Drug use among 15 year olds in Wales.* Health Promotion Authority for Wales, 1991.

Time Out. *A research report conducted with 25 year old Time Out readers.* Hallett Arendt, 1993.

Time Out. *Survey of readers.* Hallett Arendt, 1994.

How do drugs affect the family?

by Nicholas Dorn, Jane Ribbens & Nigel South

This is an account of the difficulties that have confronted a number of families facing prolonged drug problems. It is based on interviews and discussions with women and men throughout England who have gained years of experience of coping with the drug use of a relative – often a son or daughter.

Finding out about the drug use

There is a great range and mixture of emotions that may be aroused when a person first realises that their child, husband, wife or other relative or close friend is using drugs. These emotions are likely to be felt very deeply. Mothers in particular react very strongly:

> 'Anger, angry that you can't do anything. My first response was anger that he was so weak to do it – horror, horror.'

> 'The word 'heroin', I was petrified. I was terrified of even the word. The thing is not to be frightened. You can go so wrong by being scared. You just learn as you go on. I've learned not to be scared of drugs.'

> 'I think one reacts in two ways, either the family might be made tremendously angry, or they are made tremendously frightened and anxious, or a mixture of both. Some parents will be extremely aggressive about it.'

Sometimes the emotions get directed inward rather than at the child or the drug dealers so that the parents blame themselves and worry that they have failed as parents. They feel that they are guilty in some way:

---

from *Coping with a Nightmare*: *family feelings about long-term drug use.* ISDD 1995. Available from ISDD

'The chief reaction you feel is guilt, what I felt was 'what can be the matter with me?', 'what am I doing destroying my own children? The last thing I want to do and it's happening'.'

Guilt as an emotion can be a very powerful driving force, but it may or may not be a force for good. This mother felt a deep sense of responsibility for her adult married son because of his earlier childhood experiences:

'I felt responsible for Tim because I've been married three times, I think that some children can cope with broken marriages and others can't and it's just a sense of responsibility. The things that Tim's gone through probably did help him to lead the life he lived. It did have something to do with me, and that's maybe why I could help him, because I felt responsible.'

On the other hand, another mother felt that emotions of guilt just undermined her actions with her daughter, and made her give in to her on issues when she did not actually think it was right to do so:

'There's one side of you saying, well I don't know if I need to feel guilty, I did act for the best at the time, which is true. On the other hand, you look back and you can see at some time a grey area where everything hadn't gone well. So you can't bear to see them suffering as much as they are. It's a sort of emotional blackmail, really grinding you down.'

There may also be a feeling of deep loss, that all your child's promise and all your hopes for her have just come to this:

'She had the talent, it was so sickening. She's got it all there, it's so sickening.'

'It was a sense of terrible devastating loss.'

Sometimes the sense of loss combines with the feelings of anger, so that parents may feel they have been betrayed by their child:

'I just couldn't believe that this child whom I adored would actually have done that to us, I felt it was a personal betrayal really. How could she have done that to us?'

'What happens is this. A terrifying feeling of fear and a sort of desperate disappointment, you know, how can this happen – he was so lovely, my child, how can it have happened to my child?'

Again every family is unique and not everyone necessarily has such strong emotional reactions when they first become aware of a potential drug problem in their family. But the shock may come later:

'He used to tell me that his wife was on it and he wasn't and he wanted to get her out of it. Every time we used to go up there they seemed alright – he was exaggerating. When he was alright you'd think – perhaps it's not so bad. So I didn't realise then that he was on really hard stuff. It's not until I found him in such a bad condition, having fits.'

However, strong emotional reactions may not be especially helpful, although they may be very difficult to escape:

'Our doctor kept saying, keep calm and cool. Eventually I said, 'It's all very well for you to say this, but it's impossible'.'

Nevertheless, another mother echoes this doctor's advice:

'Everybody without a doubt overreacts in the first instance. Life has continued. If anything's going to happen to them it is not going to happen to them there and then.'

How does the rest of the family respond?

So far the family has been discussed as though it is all one unit, and of course this is not true. Different members of the family may react in different ways to a drug problem and they may not always have a united front in dealing with the issues. Very often it does seem to be the mothers who feel most affected by the problem and who get most involved in trying to make things better. Fathers' involvements seem to be more varied.

What about the fathers?

A number of mothers feel that their husbands are more detached from the problems, and may be less caring:

'I think a caring mum always cares, they hate to see their kids go wrong and hate to see their kids make a mess of their lives. I think some fathers find it difficult to handle the situation and they can seem to move away from it. Fathers are not as emotionally involved. A few families I've met, the fathers have found it difficult, they just cut off. They find they can't handle it, so they shut off and leave it to the mother. Or they write the kids off, they say, 'leave home'.'

Perhaps also fathers see traditional assumptions about their roles as setting up barriers to their deeper involvement. One father who now regularly attends a parents' group with his wife, was very conscious of this:

> 'There is always the barrier between two things: the mother is always going to be protective towards the child and the father is always going to be the dominant one – teaching him to do the right things and making him live up to me, not to her, as it were. She is just there to look after him. That's just how it is – now we are being sexist! – but that's the way it works and that's the way it is.'

There seems to be a suggestion that fathers do not have the range of responses that a mother may have, so that when a father finds that he cannot control his son's or daughter's drug use, he may tend to withdraw emotionally, or else to want to reject the child and remove the problem that way. Whatever kind of response fathers can make, it is this sense of lack of control over the situation that seems central. This is illustrated in the following extracts from a discussion among three fathers about the frustration that they felt in 'not being able to cope with the problem':

> 'See, as a man, when it comes to the crunch in the house, the man makes the decisions most of the time. Alright, he may be manipulated by the women in the home, but I mean the man is looked towards when it comes to the crunch. The man has to make the decisions....'

But in dealing with a young drug user in the family:

> '.....now we come to a situation where a little bit of grey comes in, because you cannot deal with the problem you have in your own house because the very person that is creating the problem isn't listening because of his drug problem.'

> 'You're so right, Fred. The difficult thing for the man to me, is really the fact that he is not able to cope with the problem but will not admit it to himself or anybody else.'

Obviously fathers feel there is something special about the position that they are placed in both emotionally and rationally. Some sense of this comes out in the thoughtful comment of one father regarding his relationship with his drug-using son:

> 'Perhaps – you've got a sort of reflection of masculine values on one side with the young man trying to prove himself, and the father perhaps responding in a way that is not understanding or not accepting this because it is not how the father would see masculine behaviour.'

A different point of view is that fathers are simply less articulate about their feelings. As one father said:

'I simply can't talk about it.'

'Women are just more able to share their feelings with other people, they don't mind so much talking about it. We find in the parents' group that men can take quite a time to sort of loosen up and say anything that really means something. In fact at one meeting when we were talking about, 'What have we all got in common?' one father ruefully said, 'They've all got mothers who talk too much'.'

The other side of the coin then, may be the argument that the mothers are too involved, too centred on the problems. Certainly a number of mothers have sought help from their doctors for the degree of stress they have felt, and may be prescribed tranquillisers as a result. This wife of a drug user can perhaps appreciate different points of view:

'A mother very often feels more sorry for the addict than the father. I think the father feels that his wife is probably suffering and he doesn't really understand it.'

An experienced drug counsellor was also aware of the different points of view:

'Some fathers really do not want to know and would instantly reject the child once they hear about the drugs problem. For example, one father came in here just the other day and said, 'Well, if there's one rotten apple in the barrel you just throw it out don't you?' And this was before there had been any sort of trauma in the family. But if fathers can remain involved they do have something extra to offer. Fathers can sometimes be a bit more objective, perhaps a bit tougher.'

One mother's interpretation of differing parental concerns was as follows:

'The fathers on the whole just did not want to know because they could not cope with the idea. It seems funny but the mothers seem to be able to cope with it, or at least seem to have to shoulder the burden .... The fathers were more concerned not about the health of the addict but that there would be trouble, that they would be picked up by the police, their address would be in the paper, people at work would know.'

Of course this may be a bit of a stereotype. Some fathers do get seriously involved in support groups. One father described how he felt bewildered and angry about the lack of male involvement in the groups that he attended:

'You know, you see predominantly mothers – there must have been, in the rooms at Riverside, about 30 women and about four men and I was still so hostile or angry that the first question I asked when I got up was, accusingly, 'Why are there so few men?' as if it was their fault. And they just said, well that is just the way it is, you know – it would be marvellous if there were more men.'

For this father, the most appropriate initial response was not to sit around talking but to organise as a group of men and literally fight the problem:

'I went along to the few men there and said, 'What are we doing here? Let's leave the mothers to discuss this bloody problem, we'll go out and get pick-axe handles and we'll find ourselves some pushers and we will smash the bloody living daylights out of them' – and thank God, everybody said, 'Dave, that just isn't the way it is – just sit and listen and maybe you'll learn'. And there were flip little things that were said that were very, very wise and profound, like 'come back for six meetings and if you're not satisfied we'll give you back your misery'. And I liked those sort of little quips and everything – so I thought, I'll keep coming back.'

This father now feels that the experience of helping his two sons through heroin addiction was such a significant period that it has changed his view of life generally.

'.... the first part of my life I operated from love and the second part I operated from fear. What this whole drug experience and coming through it has done for me is to put me back, in the last third of my life, into operating from love, not from fearing.'

So – some men do get involved, do think about their roles and do respond in a variety of ways, but they seem to be in the minority as the principal active carers.

Clearly there are different points of view between mothers and fathers about how to respond and sometimes these may relate to long-term differences between a couple. Drug problems may then bring out underlying conflicts between a husband and wife, even when the drug user is not living at home:

'How it didn't break us up I don't know. Now that Sam is away, all I get from my husband is about Sam. He says that I never told him about Sam. So still Sam is causing trouble even though he's not there. But it was always me that was up in the night. I always felt my husband didn't really care. You'd hear him snoring away upstairs. He doesn't drink a lot but if it got bad he'd go out for a pint and that was his relaxation. If I could do that ....'

Sometimes the mother may feel her loyalties become very divided:

'Don't force me to make the choice whether I'm going to go with her and help her, or stay with you, because I don't want to make that choice.'

Brothers and sisters

While so much attention is focused on the drug user, what is happening to any other children in the family?

Clearly much will depend here on the ages of the children, and whether they are younger or older than the one who is dependent on drugs. Whatever their situation, though, it seems likely that brothers and sisters also feel a variety of strong emotions about the situation, in some ways parallel to the range of emotions that have been discussed in relation to the parents:

'Anna went very shy and she couldn't relate to her age group. I think it had affected her a tremendous amount and I'm sure people don't realise how much it affects the sisters, especially if there is only one.'

There is of course the danger that other children may be rather overlooked in the stress of coping with a drug user:

'We didn't realise how much attention we were giving him. I mean, if anybody had said you're treating your children unevenly, you're paying far more attention to one than you are to the other, I think I would have said 'nonsense'. And yet it was true looking back on it. The family goes crazy, and it doesn't matter how many kids are in the family, the addict gets preferential treatment over the regular people who are not ill.'

Sisters and brothers may also have to cope with seeing their parents and their family in danger of collapsing under the strain of coping with the drug user:

'My older sons and daughter were very relieved when I found something to help me and my husband. Because what they said was, we can't bear to see what she's doing to you. Never mind about her, was their attitude, they just couldn't stand watching the two of us suffering, that made them very angry.'

'But younger brothers and sisters can get very upset. It disturbs them at school, because they hear this constant bickering – not necessarily from the addict, because the addict can turn a totally blind eye to all the upset they cause as long as they have what they want. But it causes constant quarrelling between the mother and the dad, and this in turn rubs off on the kids. And they want to ask questions, and nobody wants to answer the questions to the younger ones.'

Again, not everyone finds this such a difficulty though:

'We haven't explained it to the other kids at all. They just accepted it. All the little one needs to know is that her brother's a drug addict, and she doesn't really question it. She's only eight years old but she knows that Terry's an addict. Children are a lot cuter [more clever] than you think.'

Sometimes too, the drug user is fully aware of the effects they are having on the people around them – and that awareness may be more than they can cope with:

'I think there are times when the user is in such a state that he's done such terrible things to his family, and they do really truly feel that the only way they can get rid of that is to have another shot, and so it gets worse and worse.'

Such upsets may lead to very angry feelings towards the drug user so that brothers and sisters may want to reject their sibling:

'They tend to want to disown them because of all the upset they've caused to the parents.'

The brother or sister may also feel that they are ashamed of their whole family because they are associated with a drug user:

'She didn't want to mix with people here because of it. She didn't want to come home. She could never accept that Carol was upsetting the family, Carol was a disgrace. Anna was a bit upper crust you see, and she thought that Carol had let the family down in a big way, and our name would be mud in the village and that sort of thing. She absolutely switched off and she's just coming back into the family only now.'

With many brothers and sisters, feelings of anger may live side by side with feelings of strong affection. Sometimes, the ties between brothers and sisters may lead them to a protectiveness towards the drug user:

'Sometimes the brother or sister is the protector. They can become over-protective. One mother said when her addicted son was about 21, her nine year-old daughter was saying, don't worry mummy, I'll look after him.'

On occasions it may be that sisters or brothers together may be covering up, keeping what's going on from the parents:

'Our younger daughter had a boyfriend who was a heroin addict. We didn't know this, and he was like a second son to us. We feel quite betrayed by him now because he introduced our eldest daughter to heroin and we didn't know and our youngest daughter didn't tell us, so that this conspiracy was going on.'

There may also be the fear, (and sometimes the reality), that sisters or brothers may follow the example set and themselves start using drugs:

'The other kids, like the youngest one, when she saw him really bad, I went upstairs, she was crying. She said, 'Oh mum', she panicked, 'He's not living, he's half dead'. At least one thing – she's learned a hard lesson. I pray to God she'll never do it and yet you say that, but in the next breath she says, 'I wonder what it's like'.'

One of the things that most worries people when a son, daughter, husband, wife or other relative gets heavily involved in drugtaking is – why is this happening in our family? Is there something wrong with us, as a family? In the next section, we show how some people try to come to grips with this question.

Feeling guilty

'You never think it's going to happen to you, you never ever give it a thought. Well it's like somebody dying isn't it, well it's never going to be my husband or my children. You read about it, you pick up a paper, but it's the same with everything that happens in the world, you read and you just put the paper down and you don't think about it any more.'

Through all the issues and responses to do with illegal drug use in a family, one worry which tends to underlie many parents' feelings, is the question, was it my fault? Am I to blame for having brought up a child who has taken to using drugs? I thought it only happened in problem families.

It is very clear that a drugs problem can arise in almost any family, regardless of background or circumstances:

'It's not just kids from poor homes, or kids whose mothers are out at work all the time, or kids who are out of work. We've got kids from professional homes, young kids. It discriminates against neither colour, creed not class.'

Another mother, the wife of a prosperous business man, describes the situation with some anger:

'I heard about some judge who thought that every addict should be thrown into prison. I felt like throwing something at him. It does more harm than good. There's nowhere that's safe. Drugs go right across the spectrum, they aren't just for the poor down-and-outs or the rich. They're right across the middle class, right across the professional classes, right the way through. There is nobody who's free from it.'

In this family it was the child who was doing well at school who started to use drugs:

'He was badly misled at school. It started when he was doing 11 O-levels. There wasn't a boy in that academic stream that wasn't dabbling in speed in order to get through the swotting.'

Why do people want to take drugs? One aspect which it may be difficult to accept is that taking drugs can be pleasurable, so that the user may seem contented while those around him or her are deeply concerned:

'I mean an addict doesn't need anybody while he's got his stuff.'

'The feeling is great, they feel good, they feel all wrapped up, all warm. It takes them over completely. But it takes them over totally, and wrecks their lives. But how can you tell a child how dreadful it is until they've tried it?'

Fore-warned is fore-armed?

Whether or not a family has had any previous knowledge about drugs does not always seem to make a great deal of difference. Some parents feel that they should have given their child more warnings about drugs before they got involved with them:

'We were very un-druggy kind of people. Maybe the fact that they never had any tablets when they were little meant that it held that little bit more fascination for her – or at least provoked a sense of innocence about drugs and their seriousness.'

'As parents we are very naive, well not so much now, but I was. I mean I've even picked magic mushrooms with my daughter. I didn't know what magic mushrooms were, I didn't even know they existed.'

Many such parents advise strongly that children be educated from an early age about the dangers of drugs:

'I think they've got to keep on at their kids, keep warning them of the dangers.'

'I'm certain it's a question of education and putting it across to youngsters at a very early age. It's got to be put across to them in primary school.'

On the other hand some parents find that their children use drugs even when they have clear knowledge of the dangers, based on the experience of seeing a brother or sister who has had a history of drug abuse.

'One of the older boys in particular took LSD and actually became very disturbed and ill with it. I thought that would put all the younger ones off. They're not going to mess about with drugs seeing what it's done to him.'

But in this family two more children went on to use heroin.

Are all drugs equally serious? In some families with children who have had experience of using cannabis, parents have tried to take a serious attitude to this without over-reacting:

'Well, we knew that she smoked pot a bit, or whatever – cannabis – because everybody sort of did at that time, and one knew that. And one would warn her she couldn't do more than that.'

As another family's experience seemed to suggest, sometimes this approach may seem to work quite satisfactorily:

'When my older children were at University and so on, they smoked pot. I did know about it and I was worried about it. But I thought at the time you know, they say it's not particularly harmful so if I make a terrible fuss I will make it worse, and I sort of let it go really. And in fact they just grew out of it, which most people do.'

Blaming the drug dealers

Another feeling may be that it is the drug dealers who are to blame, making it especially difficult to realise that many users are themselves dealers. So it may be your child's friends or even your child herself who is dealing in drugs:

'We first discovered she was using drugs when she was about 14. She was going to a church youth club, and a lad that she was seeing had been found with drugs. It turned out he was using her as a go-between and selling speed and various things to kids at the grammar school.'

It's their responsibility

In the end most parents seem to believe that the young person has to be seen as responsible for his or her own actions:

'There can be underlying problems – I mean, you get people saying that it's unemployment and this and that, well, all right, people, particularly the young ones, get very low, they've got a lot of time on their hands, so it's boredom, but at the end of the day it's still down to that particular person whether they take it or not.'

'As my own daughter said, nobody said to her she must take this.'

Similarly, as will be discussed later, in the end a lot of stress is put on the drug user's own motivation wanting to come off drugs.

Did we have a bad relationship?

Nevertheless parents may worry that they have done something in the past or failed their child in some way, which had brought about a drug problem. One thing which does seem to come across quite strongly from parents, is that very often they have had what they consider to be good relationships with their children before they started using drugs, and that frequently there is the strong feeling that they were very nice people:

'He was living at home, a very nice boy, very sort of charming and affectionate.'

Some parents also feel that they have known their children's friends well and would have expected to know if any of them were starting to use illegal drugs:

'We think we were in a good position to find out as well as anybody could do, because we always had their friends into the house before they left home. We enjoyed their company and the company of their friends as well.'

On the other hand, sometimes drug use is added on to other problems that were already there, or the parents may feel that there always has been something a bit different about the child:

'He's always been outrageous, he's always been that type of boy.'

Never mind the reasons why!

In the end many people also believe that it does no good to keep worrying about the reasons why a child, or other family member or friend, has started to use drugs:

'You find strict parents, you find lackadaisical parents, you find young parents, you find old parents. Everyone starts by blaming themselves. 'It's because I was too strict', 'It's because I wasn't strict enough'. The thing is that nobody really knows why. What you've got to do is deal with the problem you now have. Perhaps one day when our son Martin is a married man with grandchildren or something, we'll sit around in this room and say, 'Have you ever thought why?' and we might have an interesting discussion and we might come to a conclusion. But if we were to have that discussion now it would mean we were dwelling on the past.'

'Did you really bring this about or didn't you, because none of us wanted it? We also think it's not productive to go on worrying about it. What we would have to do is accept the fact that it has happened, this very severe blow has befallen us. You can't unmake the past and go back to the beginning and start all over again.'

Difficult times

How do feelings change when drug use is no longer a new shock to the family system, but part of the reality of life that has to be dealt with over a period of time? What is the emotional impact of such experience? How do people cope while they are trying to come to terms with such a mixture of emotions – some of which are feelings that no parent is ever supposed to feel towards their child, even if we do all come close to some very negative feelings at times with our children.

Clearly there may be some very low times and some very distressing feelings. Parents may find themselves struggling to hold the family together:

'When our daughter was trying to commit suicide I remember saying to a doctor once, 'Let her die. Don't stop her, let her go,' because I honestly even today, I would rather see her dead than back on drugs.'

Interviewer: 'But if you'd let that doctor do what you wanted him to do she wouldn't be alive today.'

'That's right, but even so when I said that I meant it, I really did. I couldn't go back to it.'

Feelings of anger, of wanting anything rather than to have to face life with a drug-using child, and perhaps wanting to reject the child, may be common at some time:

'I told him if he goes back on drugs I don't want him. I have often wished he'd be dead or he'd have an accident so he'd end up in hospital so that someone else could see the problem and maybe take over.'

In other circumstances, the feelings of anger and rejection may be overridden by a view of the problem which hopes for some sort of merciful relief:

'I was that worried in the night when he was really bad, saying please God let him die, just let him die.'

A further point of view is that feelings of betrayal may actually be sought by the user to increase the pressure on his family to reject him:

'Parents go through a stage of saying the children are doing it to us, and whether it's deliberate or not, the addiction is being acted out against the family. Part of the addiction is a courting of a rejection by the addict. In order to get to a position where the addict feels comfortable in continuing the addiction, he needs to be rejected by the family, because that explains to him why he needs to be an addict.'

Apart from the initial crisis that may occur when parents first discover that their child is using drugs, there may be other times of particular disruption and upheaval that parents may find particularly hard to cope with. One such time may be if the young person gets arrested so that there are worries about criminal prosecutions, with all that may entail for the child and for the family:

'She was arrested twice and that was when I sort of really despaired.'

Another time of difficulty is when the person makes an attempt to come off drugs, yet fails for some reason. Some users make *several* attempts before they are successful. Parents realise that they should support every attempt by the user to stop using drugs – after all, even an unsuccessful attempt is a step forward. But when things go badly, many parents feel helpless and full of despair:

'How people react is, sometimes they almost sort of give up. There doesn't seem to be anything you can do, which is very unhelpful because the addicted person does need to feel that there is a way out ... When I look back and think how things were with my own daughter two years ago, it seems like a miracle. She's getting steadily better and happier and making wise decisions about her future. Happily lots of these miracles are walking about now.'

'What hope is there for the lad if you yourself don't keep hope.'

However one factor which may contribute to the sense of despair may be a feeling of frustration with the users themselves:

'They don't see what they're doing. We see, but they don't so you have a particularly difficult situation.'

'With a parent it's frustration more than anything because you can't do anything, it's up to them.'

Again it is sometimes thought that strong and powerful emotions may not be helpful to the parents or their child, however understandable those emotions may be:

'That's natural, natural to be angry, natural to be anxious, natural to be frightened, but you are not doing an awful lot for the recovery of that person if you allow yourself to be overwhelmed by these feelings. Try then to manage that and turn it to good account rather than allow yourself to go on being swept round and round. It's our own responsibility to control ourselves.'

Alongside the anger may be the desire to try to help in some way:

Interviewer: 'After you felt anger what was the next sort of thing you felt?'

'We wanted to help him as much as we could, and we did. We have always supported him really, apart from the rows, we've always supported him.'

This may of course be based on very deep and long-standing feelings as a parent:

'Others said 'I wouldn't have him in my house', and I'll start getting to think I should get him to leave but you can't when you're a mum. I mean all the years you bring them up. You have a healthy baby and they have all these illnesses – you've got to be there haven't you?'

'We've found through bitter experience really, that the greatest thing and the hardest thing when they're going through that drug phase is to learn to love them, because you've got to learn to love them in a way that you've never loved them before. You've really got to search yourself, you've got to find out how to love them.'

At the end of the day too, there is the necessity to survive and carry on, taking each day as it comes:

'You take each day as it comes. Don't look back, stop mulling over the past, with regret and stop anxiously hovering over the future, the fear of what will or won't happen and live in the day. Just do the best you can in that particular day. It's often all you can do. And then the best you can in the next day.'

Planning ahead for a life without drugs

'It's very important for the parents to appreciate that you can't think that you can just bung them [serious drug users] into a detoxification programme for two weeks and everything will be back to normal, because it won't. It's become a way of life with them, and they have to learn to change their whole way of life and their whole attitude.'

Most parents appreciate the difficulties that young people may face in keeping off drugs after being 'on' them for a considerable amount of time:

'I mean they can come off ... Three weeks or a month and it's over with. It's just keeping them off, and then it's finding them something hopefully to occupy them, I would say, getting an interest in something ...'

'And then what is their life going to be? I think you've got to plan ahead more or less some life and support before they want to come off because it's too big a thing to come off and have nothing. It needs a whole change of lifestyle, friends and everything. So I think there has to be a substitute ... if she doesn't change her environment and she still maintains the same friends and lives in the same place ... we can't see any chance for Sarah ...'

Some people also feel that the ex-user is likely to have a great deal of lost ground and lost time to make up:

'And she said something which I think is very true – 'I have lost six years of my life. I have got to make up for those six years. I've got to go back and start again'.'

When people get heavily into drugs – and this goes for alcohol too – the user may be involved in it as a whole way of life. Their friendships may be all based around drug use, and if their friends are still using, the ex-user may come under a good deal of pressure to start again. So staying off the drugs may require establishing a whole new way of life. Some parents have found that this is the time they seem to be most needed:

'A lot of the children, when they come off, that's who they turn to anyway, the parents again.'

This is the time when anyone trying to help the person needs to be prepared to be flexible, to try new approaches. An approach that has worked at one time (say, early on, at the start of the problem), may not be right at another time (once the drug user has built up the motivation to make a determined effort to give up).

Jobs

For one mother, keeping hold of her son's job as an apprentice became a central issue in coping with his drug use:

'I said, 'Well, he's got to get his apprenticeship'. His father said to me, 'What good is the apprenticeship if he's dead? ... you're not thinking clearly'.'

In this family, the son did eventually lose his apprenticeship, but he successfully won his fight against drugs. However, to be a drug user does not necessarily mean that a person will not be able to hold down a job. Indeed there are a number of studies of the lifestyles of users of a variety of drugs which show that they can get on with a working life very well at the same time as they are using. This is the case whether the jobs be unskilled or professional, clerical or managerial. For others however, it is not unlikely that work behaviour may fall apart just as home behaviour may do:

> 'Not everybody loses their jobs almost immediately and becomes sort of unviable. A lot of people providing they can get regular supplies can in fact continue working after a fashion ... It really doesn't look as if anything too bad is wrong, she keeps changing jobs you know.'

> 'He was painting and decorating, he was working but a very poor job record, in and out of jobs.'

Sometimes during periods of recovery parents may be concerned to build up work habits again:

> 'I got her a part-time job in the drycleaners, not telling them anything about her problem. I jolly well made sure myself that she was there at half past eight every morning ... I never let her go on the dole ever, I said if you go on the dole I'll have between £15 and £18 of that for keeping you, so you can forget you're going to have any money because I'm going to have that, and you'll have a job.'

This may have the bonus of allowing the person to make a real contribution so that they can feel valued:

> 'Then she went to a nursing home, she ... is so good with old people and they adored her. She went back to a home where she used to work, and the person who ran the home knew that she had a problem and she was super, she said, 'Come on Carol, if you're promising me you are going to be okay, I'll have you back, I loved having you, so come back', and she did.'

Trying to make some sense of it

Many parents say how bewildered they feel when they find they have a drug problem in the family, because it is not like anything else they have come across, either in their own young days or amongst other parents that they know. So how do people try to make sense of the issue – what sort of a problem is it?

The period when a young person is developing independence from the family is fraught with tensions for both the young person and the parents. For the young person, there are the tensions of wanting to establish herself as an independent and self-determining individual, yet not quite sure if she is ready to leave the security of childhood. The parents are caught between the tensions on the one hand of trying to let them go and allow them to take responsibility for their own lives, and yet on the other hand feeling deep concern to support them or even direct them when they seem to be stumbling. We can see all these tensions greatly magnified in the context of drug problems. One view is that it is much like other forms of teenage experimentation:

'We had a very good headmaster who used to say that in the town there were three problems, drugs, alcohol and sex, and he reckoned you never had any two at the same time. They used to experiment. I'm absolutely certain he is right that children will experiment. They start through their friends because they want to be one of the boys.'

However, as well as a striving for independence through rebellion and experimentation to be part of the teenage group, to some parents drug use looks more like a search for security – children trying to avoid the pain of growing up and facing the realities of adult life:

'In a way, you can imagine it being like a return to the womb, the security that you have in the womb, the warmth. It blanks out everything that hurts you. They are pathetic really. I mean when they get to the state she was in, I mean, she would come home and she would just curl up, she was like a little girl again.'

One father came to see the drug problem in his family as being like old fairy stories where the young person is put to the test and has to overcome great terrors in order to win through to new opportunities:

'You know, where young people are sent to kill dragons, and overcome witches, and hack their way through the forest. And when they've met all their tests they went through to the sleeping princess. And that is true not only for the addicts but also in a funny way for parents, loved ones. They are given an opportunity to transform their lives. It's a very hard test to face, but this is reality. I suddenly find that my life has opened up.'

For one mother, herself now of retiring age, who has been supporting her son for a long time without much change in the situation, a very different comparison seems to be relevant:

'He's 35, he's a man, and we keep saying that, you know, he should be making his own way in life. But he's been damaged. I mean if we'd had a mentally handicapped child – but this is different.'

To some people it is simply a self-inflicted problem. Doctors seem especially likely to take this view – perhaps because they also see so many problems that are so clearly totally out of the control of the sufferer concerned. But some parents also seem to take a view that drug use is a sign of weakness, a sort of character defect:

'I don't think it's necessary that he has to rely on drugs to cope with life.'

There is also of course the legal aspect to many forms of drug use, and the overtones of criminality:

'Generally parents don't want to see their kids go wrong, it's just like any crime or anything isn't it? It's no way of life for kids living on drugs, they can't have a decent way of life on drugs.'

This may also of course contribute to parents' feelings of shame that were discussed earlier:

'The feeling of shame that I had. She'd been arrested. The awful shame and grief I'd felt.'

'You've got to forget your pride, you've got to put your pride behind you. They shouldn't be ashamed of their sons and their daughters or their husbands or whoever it is, just try to put that behind and seek some help.'

'There's one thing you find when you know you've got an addict in the family, and that is shame and you can't tell anybody. I myself used to look upon addicts as simply scum.'

As well as feelings of shame, very strong feelings of anger and hurt are experienced. The person the family loved has let them down so badly, and perhaps acted in ways that are felt to be cruel. It can be very difficult to accept this, and to reconcile with the person the family thought they knew. One way some parents have tried to cope with this, is to see the drug user as almost two-people-in-one:

'I think one thing that might help which certainly helped me, what came to me was the fact that the person you are dealing with whilst they are using drugs is not your son or daughter or husband. If you can sort of look at them apart, separate them. Imagine them as they were before they used drugs, and look at the person that you know, and when the person has stopped using they're back to that person again. It is the drug itself that is making them do all the things they are doing. If you look at it like that it doesn't hurt so much.'

One fairly widespread view is that heavy drug use, like alcoholism, is an illness. While this may be a matter for continuing debate, many people say they find it very helpful to see it this way, since it removes some of the feelings of blame and guilt and allows for hope of a cure:

'We don't take any sort of a moral line about it at all. Just take the line that it is an illness. If we treat it like that it seems to be much simpler, the whole situation sort of simplifies. You can get rid of a whole lot of emotions that are unhelpful, like guilt and anger.'

'Once you look on addiction as an illness and not as a moral issue you're halfway there. Because suddenly all the shame and guilt and everything goes.'

On the other hand, there may be a point where this analogy seems to break down:

'In our parents' support group, there we were with sick children. But whereas when they were kids and they had measles or a cold or ear infection and you knew exactly what to do to help them through that sickness, here we were faced with a sick child and totally incapable of bringing them any help at all, other than by doing the naughty things we occasionally did – like buying them a bottle of codeine or giving them an extra fiver, knowing damn well that the extra fiver was to go on a fix.'

At the same time many family members also stress that drug users, like anybody else, can be very nice people:

'It does take a lot of understanding, believe me, because when they're on drugs they're cold, they're callous, they're horrible. But in the end they end up hating themselves for that. They really are very caring people, very sensitive people. They seem to want to look at the world and then can't take what they see.'

'Without the drug he is a marvellous person and I think most people can say that. I'm sure if they'd only gone the other way, I think they could have been quite something.'

A number of ex-users do go on to help others who are trying to stop using drugs, and may become very involved in this way. Some parents also find that listening to ex-users can be very helpful when they are trying to understand what is going on within their own family:

'I had invaluable support from Terry, an ex-addict. I would tell him about what was going on with my daughter, and he would say, 'Oh don't worry it's because ...' He would explain what she would be feeling, and we found ourselves thinking, it isn't her, she's not such an oddball, it's recognised behaviour, and he was just an enormous help and support.'

'Junkies that I have come across have greater insight into what they are doing than most people seem to recognise, and are interested and will sit for hours and hours, just discussing what is going on and why.'

Over the years

Some people we talked to had experienced a drug problem in their family or had been helping other families over several years. How had they adapted to it as a family over a long period of time?

'From experience I can say that once you know you've got an addict, or even an ex-addict, your peace of mind is gone. I know a person whose son's been off drugs for three years, and still every time they go out, they're worried. Because it's so easy for an addict to go back onto drugs.'

'It'll be five years in November and I'm still wondering. I can't honestly say I know one hundred per cent she's off drugs because I don't, I really don't.'

'The difficulty I find is not so much the coming off the drugs, it's the staying off the drugs. That's the long haul, and parents have got to have so much more courage, so much more patience.'

However the same parents who are speaking here also have some very positive comments to make:

Father: 'Our family is different than it was before – the quality of life now is better than before.'

Mother: 'We've learned a lot through it haven't we?'

Drugs and Crime:

Drug use and criminal behaviour

by Trevor Bennett

It is widely believed that there is an association between drug use and criminal behaviour. This belief is based on the results of a substantial body of academic research which has shown that drug use and criminal behaviour are related. This belief is also based on popular wisdom as revealed in the stereotype of the drug-crazed addict who will stop at nothing to obtain drugs or money for drugs. However, the wealth of evidence supporting a drugs-crime connection belies a poverty of knowledge in our understanding of this association.

The problem can best be explained by making a distinction between a 'statistical connection' between drug use and crime and a 'causal connection'. The former concerns whether drug use and criminal behaviour are found together – either in the same place or in the same individual. The latter concerns whether drug use and criminal behaviour are related to one another in any kind of meaningful or causal way.

There is a great deal of evidence on the 'statistical connection' which has lead to some (but not full) agreement that there is a relationship between drug use and crime. There is much less evidence available on the 'causal connection'. Until the nature of the relationship between drug use and criminal behaviour is understood the evidence of a statistical association is of little importance and has limited policy implications.

---

from *The International Handbook of Addictive Behaviour* edited by Ilana Belle Glass, Routledge 1991

The statistical connection

Research on the statistical association between drug use and crime uses three main methods of investigation. The first is referred to here as studies of 'national and regional trends' which examine the relationship between broad movements in drug use and broad movements in crime. The second is referred to as studies of 'drug-using criminals' which examine drug use among samples of criminals. The third is referred to as studies of 'criminal drug users' which examine criminal behaviour among addicts and other drug users. The words 'drug' and 'drug use' are used in this chapter to refer mainly to heroin and other opioid drugs.

National and regional trends

The relationship between crime and drug use was investigated by the 'ecological school' of Chicago sociologists during the 1930s, who argued that criminal behaviour and other social problems (including drug use) tended to be concentrated in certain areas of the city. The general findings of these studies supported their theories and showed that high rates of addiction were associated with high rates of crime and delinquency. Later studies conducted in New York City in the 1950s confirmed these early findings showing that drug use was most frequently found in areas of the city which had high crime rates.

A common method of investigating the drugs-crime connection using aggregated data is to examine the relationship between the price of heroin and crime. Studies of this kind are based on a number of assumptions about the demand for heroin. First they assume that the demand for heroin is fairly inelastic and will be unaffected by price. Second, they assume that the higher the cost of heroin the greater the amount of money needed by the pool of addicts to purchase the drug.

According to this research the relationship between heroin use and criminal behaviour can be observed by monitoring what happens during a price rise in heroin. If a rise in the price of heroin is not associated with a rise in criminal behaviour it would be assumed that addicts financed their drug use through legitimate means and that there was no evidence of a drugs-crime connection. Research which has used this technique has tended to show that there is a correlation between the price of heroin and rates of 'income-generating' crimes.

Another technique of assessing the relationship between drug use and crime is to ask experts for their opinions. The findings of these studies are sometimes referred to as 'informed guesses' or 'best estimates'. The most common method used is to mail a questionnaire to a large number of 'professionals' or 'experts' working in the field of crime or drugs (senior police officers or hospital consultants) and to ask them what percentage of criminal behaviour they believe is drug-related. The findings of this research are remarkably similar to those obtained by more rigorous methods. Professionals tend to believe that between one-third and one-half of property crimes are drug-related.

Drug-using criminals

Studies of drug use among criminals are usually based on samples of prisoners or samples of arrestees. Research conducted in prisons and other correctional institutions in the United States report a high proportion of drug users among imprisoned offenders. Some North American studies have reported that between 50 per cent and 75 per cent of all prisoners were heroin users at the time of conviction. More typical estimates are that around one-third of all prisoners have used heroin at least once in their lifetime and fewer than 20 per cent are regular users. There are no reliable figures published on drug use among British prisoners although estimates suggest that the proportions are much lower than those shown by the North American research.

Other studies which aim to determine the proportion of drug users among criminals focus on arrestees. The usual research method is to interview or to conduct urine tests on a consecutive sample of individuals arrested by the police. Research of this kind conducted in the United States has shown that about one-quarter of arrestees either admit to recent drug consumption or produce a drugs-positive urine test.

Criminal drug users

Another group of studies provide evidence on the drugs-crime connection by drawing on samples of known addicts and determining by various means their involvement in criminal behaviour.

The most common method of this group of studies is to determine the proportion of particular samples of addicts who have been convicted for at least one criminal offence. The aim of this type of research is to arrive at an estimate of 'prevalence' of offending – in other words, the percentage of the population of addicts who have at least one criminal conviction. The bulk of this research shows that the majority of regular opioid users receive at least one criminal conviction in their lifetime. Studies which compare the prevalence of conviction among opioid users and the prevalence of conviction among the general population show that opioid users are much more likely to be convicted of a criminal offence.

Another method is to determine the proportion of drug users who admit recent offending based on self-reports. These studies show, not surprisingly, that almost all addicts interviewed admit that they have committed some kind of drug offence (eg, possession or supply) during a recent period prior to the interview. More surprisingly, these studies show that between one-third and two-thirds of addicts admit to some kind of property offence (eg, shoplifting, theft, burglary). One study which was conducted from a 'store front' in East and Central Harlem found that 40 per cent of the street opioid users admitted committing a burglary within the last

28 days and 60 per cent admitted committing at least one act of shoplifting (Johnson *et al* 1985).

The timing of the onset of drug use and the onset of criminal behaviour is important as it tells us not only about the relationship between drug use and crime but also something about the potential causal ordering of the two events. The usual method is to compare official records of first criminal conviction with either official records concerning the onset of drug use or self-reported first drug use. These studies show that a high proportion of drug users had a criminal conviction prior to drug use. A Home Office study of English addicts showed that about one-third of males had been convicted prior to first admitted drug use and about half had been convicted before first opioid use (Mott and Taylor, 1974).

Some studies look at the association between periods on and off drug use and periods on and off criminal behaviour. One method is to look at the arrest rate of opioid users when they are using drugs regularly and during periods of abstention. Most of these studies show much higher arrest rates during periods of drug consumptions than during periods of abstention.

The relationship between treatment of drug addicts and criminal behaviour is important from the point of view of treatment policy. It is hoped that addicts in treatment will not only abstain from drugtaking following completion of the programme but also abstain from criminal behaviour. The results of research relevant to this problem has produced contradictory findings. Studies of this kind sometimes compare prescription groups with non-prescription groups in terms of reported criminal behaviour. The results of these studies show either that the prescription groups have lower criminal behaviour scores or that there is no difference between the two groups. Another method is to compare the criminal behaviour of users in treatment with those not in treatment or to compare the criminal behaviour of users prior to treatment with the rates for the same individuals after treatment. Research of this kind sometimes shows that treatment is associated with lowering offending rates and sometimes shows no difference in offending rates.

It is interesting to speculate on whether drug users who retire or 'mature out' of addiction also retire from crime. There are no studies to my knowledge which address this issue. Research of this kind would be useful in determining the long-term association between drug use and criminal behaviour and might provide some insights into the causal connection between the two variables.

The causal connection

Research on the nature of the relationship between drug use and crime has focused on three kinds of association: the first is referred to here as 'drug use directly causes crime'; the second is referred to as 'drug use indirectly causes crime'; and the third is referred to as 'drug use and crime are interconnected'.

Drug use directly causes crime

There are relatively few writers who argue that drug use directly causes crime. This explanation is more common in the alcohol and crime literature which argues that alcohol use can cause disinhibition which can cause the release of anti-social tendencies.

Pharmacological explanations are rare in the drugs and crime literature. It has been argued that opioid use can lead to a destruction of the character of the user which might lead to forms of behaviour that might otherwise have been considered unacceptable by the user. It has also been argued that any kind of depressant drug can lead to the same kind of disinhibition experienced under the influence of alcohol. However, there are few convincing explanations of the way in which opioid use leads directly to the motivation to commit property crimes.

Drug use indirectly causes crime

There are many more explanations of the relationship based on the idea that drug use indirectly causes crime. The main explanation of this connection is referred to as the 'economic necessity' argument.

The economic necessity argument is that addicts are forced to commit crimes to support their drugtaking habits. It is argued that regular heroin users have to spend large sums of money (often quoted at between £50 and £100 a day) to pay for drugs on the black market. As many of these users are not in full-time or well-paid employment they must be funding their habits by illegal means.

Proponents of the 'economic necessity' argument provide evidence for their view by pointing to the disparity between estimates of addicts' incomes and the costs of financing an opioid habit. The results of this research are generally impressive in their accounting skills and tend to show marked disparities between estimated costs and estimated incomes.

The findings of some of the research already mentioned is also used to support the economic necessity argument. The research shows that addicts who receive opioids on prescription tend to report lower offending rates than those not on prescription. It also shows that addicts commit fewer offences during periods of abstinence than during periods of drug use. It is believed that these findings show that when addicts no longer need to purchase drugs on the black market they no longer need to commit property crimes.

Other research provides competing evidence. One North American study showed that addicts have a number of economic options open to them apart from theft. Some income can be raised as a result of selling drugs to other addicts. Addicts might raise funds from state benefits, from contributions from family and friends and from begging and hustling.

Research conducted in this country shows that some addicts do continue to commit offences after receiving a prescription (Bennett and Wright, 1986). Some of the addicts interviewed admitted that their reasons for offending were unrelated to financing their addiction. Another writer has argued that the 'enslavement theory' that users are forced into a life of crime in order to support their habits is too simplistic (Inciardi, 1981). He points out that many addicts are involved in crime before becoming addicted and many addicts continue offending while in receipt of free drugs or while in receipt of an income from legitimate employment.

Drug use and crime are interconnected

This argument is based on the proposition that drug taking immerses the drug taker into a deviant world on the borderline of legal and illegal activity. In order to become an addict it is necessary to have access to drugs which for most users must be through dealers and other contacts on the borderline of the criminal world. It has been argued that some prior contact with criminality is a necessary condition of drug use for many addicts.

Criminality and addiction might also be interconnected because certain psychological or sociological conditions produce a propensity towards general deviance (rather than criminality or drug use) and that this general deviant disposition might lead to a wide range of rule-breaking behaviours. Evidence for this view can be found in the research which shows that many drug users have prior criminal convictions before they begin drug use.

Conclusions

The results of this body of research show that there is some evidence of a statistical relationship between drug use and criminal behaviour. It is perhaps too much to say at this stage that the evidence is overwhelming as the research providing this evidence is largely a hotchpotch of mainly small-scale studies with varying research designs.

The results of this body of research are less informative about the nature of the relationship (assuming that there is one). There is some evidence for the view that drug use causes a financial problem for some users which can only be resolved by criminal pursuits. There is also some evidence that drug users commit crimes for reasons unrelated to their addiction.

It is possible that drug use may lead to criminal behaviour among those who would not have otherwise committed an offence during their lifetime. It is more likely, however, that individuals who become involved in drugtaking are the same individuals who become involved in criminal behaviour. At this stage the most realistic conclusion seems to be that drug use exacerbates criminal behaviour rather than creates criminals.

References

Bennett, T.H. and Wright, R. (1986) 'The impact of prescribing on the crimes of opioid users', *British Journal of Addiction* 81: 265-73.

Inciardi, J.A. (1981) *The Drugs/Crime Connection*, Beverly Hills, CA: Sage.

Johnson, B.D. *et al.* (1985) *Taking Care of Business: The Economics of Crime by Heroin Abusers*, Lexington: Lexington Books.

Mott, J. and Taylor, M. (1974) *Delinquency Amongst Opiate Users*, Home Office Research Study No. 23, London: HMSO.

The cost of heroin-related crime

by Oswin Baker, Nicholas Dorn & Toby Seddon

The relationship between drugs and crime is central to some very high profile policy debates, whether as a 'cause of crime' to be tough on (or not) or as a major 'social cost' which some claim tips the balance in favour of legalisation or more liberal prescribing. It is also a relationship drug workers often view with unease: if the link is *too* strong, all drug users can be tarred with the 'thieving' brush – but if it is denied, one possible mitigating factor is lost and drug users who commit crimes are more likely to be treated simply as criminals.

The Central Drugs Coordination Unit asked ISDD to calculate the cost of heroin-related crime in England and Wales. Previously, the most recent (and widely remarked upon) calculation was that of the Greater Manchester Police, from whose work others had extrapolated that half of acquisitive crime by value in England and Wales is committed by opiate or cocaine addicts.[1] ISDD found this estimate was founded on a number of faulty assumptions:

First, it was based on an overestimate of heroin consumption (each addict taking a gram a day) so overestimated the financial needs of heroin users.

Secondly, it made no allowance for the fact that some (probably most) heroin purchases are funded by means other than acquisitive crime.

Thirdly, it relied solely on Home Office notifications of heroin addicts, so underestimated the number of dependent heroin users.

from *Druglink*, 9(6), November/December 1994, p.15

If, for instance, it had been assumed that there are twice as many dependent heroin users as are notified to the Home Office (at the lower end of the ratios usually employed), then the same calculations would have meant that 100 per cent of acquisitive crime by value was attributable to dependent heroin users! If there are five times as many addicts (at the top end of the ratio), then 250 per cent of the value of acquisitive crime is committed by heroin users. Clearly, this is impossible.

Bearing in mind these problems, ISDD set out to recalculate values or ranges of values for:

• the number of dependent heroin users in England and Wales;
• the quantity of heroin consumed by each user;
• the cost of that heroin per user;
• the multiplier for the value of stolen property sold by the user;
• the percentage of heroin users' incomes derived from acquisitive crime.

All these factors were calculable from English and Welsh data, with the exception of the last one. To get a basis for estimating this we had to look to Scotland, Holland, Germany and America.[2] We assumed that the situation in England and Wales fell somewhere within the range for these other countries – where between 16 and 48 per cent of a heroin user's income is reported to come from acquisitive crime.

Our new estimates for England and Wales were based on the following assumptions:

• the number of dependent heroin users is between twice and five times the number notified to the Home Office (the range conventionally used);
• on average, each of these users (who also typically use other drugs) consumes one third of a gram of 'street' heroin on 228 days of the year;[3]
• the price of this heroin approximates to the retail prices collated by enforcement agencies (£50-£100 a gram);[4]
• stolen property is sold for only a third of its value;
• between 16 and 48 per cent of the cost of heroin is financed by acquisitive crime.

On this basis, dependent heroin users in England and Wales raise *between £58 million and £864 million* from acquisitive crime in order to purchase heroin. Which end of this wide range is closest to reality depends on:

• whether there are two or five times as many dependent heroin users as are notified;
• whether their heroin costs them £50 or £100 per gram; and
• whether 16 or 48 per cent of their cash income comes from acquisitive crime.

This estimate amounts to *between one and 21 per cent* of the total cost of acquisitive crime in England and Wales.[5] With such poor data, a more accurate estimate cannot be made. What *is* clear is that the widely quoted estimate that half of all acquisitive crime in England and Wales is due to heroin users' need to purchase heroin is no longer tenable.

References

1. Greater Manchester Police. *Drugs/crime working group.* 1992.

Labour Party. *Drugs: the need for action.* 1994.

2. Hammersley R. *et al.* The relationship between crime and opioid use. *British Journal of Addiction*: 1989, *84*, p1029-43.

Grapendaal M. Cutting their coat according to their cloth: economic behaviour of Amsterdam opiate users. *International Journal of the Addictions*: 1992, *27* (4), p487-501.

Kreuzer A. *et al.* Perspectives on drug users. *In* Kube E. and Storzer H. eds. *Police research in the Federal Republic of Germany.* Berlin: Springer-Verlag, 1991, p151-162.

Johnson *et al. Taking care of business: the economics of crime by heroin users.* Massachusetts: Lexington Books, 1985.

Deschenes E. Anglin M. Speckart G. Narcotics addiction: related criminal careers, social and economic costs. *Journal of Drug Issues*: 1991, *21* (2), p383-411.

3. Hartnoll R. Lewis R. *The illicit heroin market in Britain: towards a preliminary estimate of national demand.* Quoted in: Home Office. *Economic aspects of the illicit drug market and drug enforcement policies in the United Kingdom.* 1988.

4. From NCIS, cited in: Baker O., Marsden J. *Drug Misuse in Britain 1994.* ISDD, 1995.

5. According to the police, in 1992 the estimated cost of all acquisitive crime in England and Wales was £4019 million. See: Home Office. *Criminal statistics, England and Wales 1992.* HMSO 1993, tables 2.18 and 2.20.

The arguments for and against legalising prohibited drugs

by Harry Shapiro

After stewing on the political back burner for some 20 years, the issue of liberalising drug laws has re-emerged on the international policy agenda, to the point where recently the UN International Narcotics Control Board felt the need to refute the arguments in its annual report.[1]

Traditionally the debate has centred on the laws relating to cannabis. Between 1968 and 1972 government-appointed committees in Britain,[2] Canada[3] and the USA[4] concluded that the medical evidence did not justify the severity of the penalties for cannabis possession. In 1979 the UK Advisory Council on the Misuse of Drugs made similar recommendations[5] as did the South Australian Royal Commission into the Non-Medical Use of Drugs.[6]

This article will review some more recent international developments and then tease out the major threads in the debate. Before that we need to look at one apparent block to nations going it alone with any decriminalisation.

The Convention

One reason why more radical law reform proposals have been dismissed is the value placed on maintaining international solidarity in the fight against drug misuse. All the major industrialised nations of the West are among the 109 signatories to the 1961 UN Single Convention on Narcotic Drugs which obliges signatories to make possession and other drug-related activities involving a range of drugs (heroin, cocaine, cannabis, etc) "punishable offences".

from *Druglink,* 9 (1), January/February 1994

This has been interpreted to mean no major relaxation of the drug laws is possible unless the nation concerned opts out of the convention. However, the official commentary to the convention is clear that nations have wide latitude in the interpretations of this provision as it applies to possession. Some have taken it that "possession" refers only to possessing the drug in the course of drug trafficking, not personal use; others have deemed fines "or even censure" as punishment enough for simple possession. So while the convention is an obstacle to the legal possession and supply of currently illicit drugs, it appears that it is no barrier to the imposition of only minor penalties for possession. Signatories need consider imprisonment only for "serious offences".[7] Several legislatures have used this flexibility to mould the convention's provisions to their own local cultures and legal systems.

In Holland, the 1976 Opium Act tripled the penalties for dealing – but an administrative framework was established which allowed the *de facto* legalisation of possession. For cannabis only, the drug was allowed to be sold from designated premises. Recently Holland has come under intense pressure to revise its policies.

The Spanish and Italian authorities have given the possession provision of the UN convention its most liberal interpretation. In Spain personal possession of any drug is not a criminal offence. In 1993, Italy reverted to punishing possession of drugs for personal use only by 'administrative' sanctions.

In the '70s 11 US states reduced penalties for personal possession of cannabis. Alaska allowed cultivation for personal use and held that it would be unconstitutional to bar its citizens from smoking cannabis in their own homes.

It is in America that the legalisation battle lines have been drawn most prominently. In the 1980s despite an ever-increasing budget, law enforcement agencies failed to stop widespread use of cocaine and the violence and massive profits for organised crime that followed in its wake.

Probably the cocaine issue more than any other prompted a catholic spread of opinion (including academics, journalists, politicians, lawyers and law enforcement officers of both liberal and conservative persuasion) to argue that US drug policy had to be reconsidered. Their motivations are as disparate as their professional interests – from civil liberties and reducing social and legal harms caused by prohibitionist laws to crime prevention.

Preventing the spread of HIV as a rationale for liberalising drug laws has not been a major feature of the American debate. However, it has been thoroughly integrated into the European debate which has seen the formation of pan-European organisations dedicated either to the rolling back of the drug laws or to their maintenance and strengthening.

The arguments

The debate is complex – more than simply a question of 'Do we legalise or not?' What degree of reform are we talking about? What is the likely impact on society of the different options? How many more people would use drugs? At what point would this increase be unacceptable? Should the opportunity also be taken to rationalise controls on alcohol and tobacco? The list goes on ...

The arguments generally break down into four areas:

• the freedom of the individual versus the duty of the state;
• the perceived harms caused by enforcing current laws;
• how a legalised control regime would work;
• the potential health harms consequent on drugs being more freely available.

The major themes in these areas are outlined below.

1. The individual and the state

The individual is entitled to conduct him or herself any way they wish so long as no harm is done to others. This principle of personal choice is applied to a wide range of private activities and should also apply to the drug use. If harm is caused by drug use (eg, harm to family, committing crimes, etc) the state can rightfully act against that harm, but not against drug use per se.

The state has a duty to protect its citizens – even from themselves. Witness the laws relating to seat belts and motorcycle helmets. Government must look to the greatest good of the greatest number even at the expense of personal liberty. Society cannot possibly benefit from maximising the chances of its citizens becoming intoxicated. And if drug use is supposed to be a matter of 'personal choice' – how much choice does the drug addict have?

2. The harm from current laws

The worst aspect of prohibition is is the way it hits the user. Many have been saddled with criminal records or even sent to prison just for possessing drugs. Enforcement of the drug laws causes tensions between the police and otherwise law-abiding citizens – especially in the sensitive area of race relations. Users have to come into contact with criminal networks to obtain drugs. Prohibition brings in its wake violence and corruption on a huge scale while making massive profits for organised crime.

Anybody who uses illegal drugs knows the price of getting caught. People have to take responsibility for their actions. Decriminalisation – legalising possession for personal use – might be even *more* damaging than legalisation. It would do nothing to undermine the illicit market while introducing more people to drugs. Users would still have to contact criminals to get their drugs – it's just that there would be more of both.

For all the billions spent on enforcement, it doesn't work – use of illegal drugs is going up all the time.

Despite their faults, the laws against drug use prevent even *more* people becoming involved.

3. How would it work?

Legalisation would transfer huge revenues to government by way of taxation on what would then be legal commodities, while wiping out the illegal market and all the problems it brings. Eradicating the illegal market would also bring enormous savings in the costs of enforcement, criminal justice and imprisonment.

Many Western governments are wedded to the merits of free market forces and know how difficult it is to 'buck' the markets. Yet they unrealistically believe they can use the law to suppress the illicit market in drugs.

How realistic is it to imagine drug syndicates would melt away if drugs were legalised? Given the prevailing economic and political ethos of the West, it is most unlikely that legalised drugs would become state monopolies. The drug business would become just another lucrative legal investment for organised crime – much as now happens in the entertainment industry (gambling, hotels, etc).

A legal market would ensure that users were getting drugs produced under proper manufacturing conditions with quality control, etc.

Illegal manufacturers will still sell adulterated products because these will be cheaper than the legal alternatives, which will almost certainly be highly taxed to curb use. For example, unlike tobacco, cannabis can be grown anywhere, so there is every chance that the illicit market will continue, undercutting heavily taxed legal suppliers.

We would be able to control legal supply more easily than illegal supply and stop drugs reaching the young or vulnerable. An unregulated market would be replaced by a regulated one.

The reform lobby goes on about legalisation without answering practical questions like: Which drugs? Who is going have access to what? How do you control manufacture and distribution, the time and place of sales, marketing and sales to minors, etc? And how successful have we been at stopping alcohol and tobacco being used by the young?

4. Health impact

Whatever health harms might be caused by drugs, the harms caused by the drug laws are much worse. We can only improve the situation by legalising.

What if you were wrong? After legalisation it would be very difficult to cut consumption, however disastrous the result. A ban could be re-imposed, but many people who had been introduced to drugs during the legal period would carry on using them. We would be in a worse position than before.

More availability doesn't equal more use – cannabis use did not escalate in the US states which decriminalised the drug in the '70s. Nor does more availability mean more addiction. During the Vietnam war many US soldiers used heroin regularly; most stopped when they returned. Heroin was easy to obtain, but the main reason soldiers used it was because they were in a war situation. Once they got home, they didn't use it even though they could have done so.

That's wishful thinking. More availability does mean more use and that means more problems. What the Vietnam experience shows is that when drugs are freely available, more people will use them, and more will become addicted. You only have to look at the numbers who smoke and drink as opposed to those who use illegal drugs to know this must be true. Then look at the massive problems we already have from tobacco and alcohol. There is good evidence that the more alcohol drinkers there are, the more become problem drinkers.

What constitutes a dangerous drug is simply a value judgement that changes across cultures and eras. At various times since the Middle Ages, drinkers of alcohol and coffee and smokers of tobacco have been subjected to draconian punishments for their indulgences. At the same time, cannabis, heroin and cocaine had (and still do have) legitimate medical uses.

The laws against drugs reflect the fact that people can get into serious health and social problems with drugs like heroin and cocaine far quicker than with alcohol and tobacco. It is a major flaw in the argument for blanket legalisation to treat all drugs the same. There are significant pharmacological differences between drugs and to suggest, for example, that crack is the same as coffee is ridiculous.

Despite our knowledge of their harmful effects, alcohol and tobacco are freely available – why not other drugs?

Even if illegal drugs were 'only' as harmful as alcohol and tobacco, why make even more harmful drugs available?

The attempt to ban alcohol in America in the 1920s was a prime example of how the law harmed people's health. Many died through drinking 'bathtub gin' and other poorly made alcoholic drinks.

From a public health point of view, Prohibition was more successful than generally assumed. The number of heavy users fell as did the incidence of cirrhosis – only to rise when alcohol was re-legalised.

Given credible information, people will avoid using drugs they believe are dangerous, just as many have reacted to the knowledge that smoking can kill.

So it seems particularly invidious to encourage the use of other smokable drugs, such as cannabis. This could undo the good that has been done through anti-smoking education.

By making cannabis illegal and treating it the same as heroin and cocaine, we undermine the credibility of drug education in the eyes of young people.

Any government legalising cannabis would be sending out the message to society that intoxication is OK.

References

1. United Nations International Narcotics Control Board. *Annual Report 1992*. 1993.

2. UK Advisory Committee on Drug Dependence. *Cannabis* (Wootton Report). 1968.

3. Canada. *Commission of Inquiry into the Non-Medical use of Drugs. Cannabis* (Le Dain Report). 1972.

4. USA. *National Commission on Drug Abuse. Marihuana – a signal of misunderstanding* (Shafer Report). 1972.

5. UK Advisory Council on the Misuse of Drugs (unpublished 1979).

6. South Australian Royal Commission into the Non-Medical Use of Drugs. *Final Report*. 1979.

7. United Nations. *Commentary on the Single Convention on Narcotic Drugs*. 1973.

European drug renegades

In general, European countries toe the accepted line on implementing international drug conventions, but there are some notable exceptions – Holland, Italy, Spain and, briefly, Switzerland.

Holland

Since the Opium Act of 1976, although possession offences have remained on the statute book, personal possession of drugs has been *de facto* decriminalised through local law enforcement directives which have in effect instructed the police to look the other way. For cannabis, Holland has gone one step further and allowed the drug to be sold in cafés.

Now there are hundreds of such premises and pressure is mounting on the Dutch Health Ministry to dismantle the arrangement. This pressure comes both from the Dutch Ministry of Justice and from Holland's European neighbours, which accuse the Dutch of encouraging 'drug tourism'. France (which takes a particularly hard line on drugs) has refused to ratify the Schengen Convention creating a 'borderless' region in Europe because of the situation in Holland. The International Narcotics Control Board has criticised Dutch policy as in contravention of the Single Convention on Narcotic Drugs.

It is unlikely that the Dutch will reverse their policy but they may introduce a licensing system, carry out checks to make sure that only cannabis is available from the 'cafes' and not (as rumoured) heroin, ecstasy and other drugs, and try to limit sales to Dutch nationals to stem the influx of drug users across the border.

Italy

Until 1990 possession of moderate amounts of drugs for personal use was not a punishable offence in Italy. Then the Socialist Premier of the day, Bettino Craxi, started an anti-drug crusade. In 1990 the law was changed to make possession punishable by penal sanctions if the amount of the drug exceeded the 'average daily dose' established in the law. Below this level 'administrative' sanctions (like confiscation of driving licences or passports) were applied, though the user could instead agree to rehabilitation. The low level of the average daily dose meant that soon the prisons and the criminal justice system were overburdened by drug use cases with no evidence that the drug problem was being lessened.

In a referendum in 1993 there was majority support for making possession of drugs for personal use in whatever quantities subject only to administrative sanctions. As before, these would be waived if the user agreed to rehabilitation. Criminal sanctions would be applied only to those convicted of more serious offences.

Spain

Since the end of the Franco era the main sanction against possession has been fines. However, opinion polls in Spain have shown most respondents favour tighter controls. Some cities have introduced a ban on drug consumption in public and there are plans in Madrid for hefty increases in fines.

Switzerland

In 1989, to curb the spread of HIV among drug users, the city of Zurich supplied free needles and syringes to users who were then allowed to inject in a city park 'exclusion zone' unmolested by the police. However, the number of users soared and in the wake of dealing and violence, the experiment ended in 1992.

United Kingdom

In its own way the UK has for decades been an international drug renegade. A selected band of doctors are allowed to stretch their clinical discretion far enough to prescribe injectable heroin and smokable cocaine to addicts. This dent in the demonology of heroin – implying that even addicts can benefit from the drug – has at times irritated other nations whose laws are framed on the assumption that the drug has no legitimate uses.

A live debate

In Britain today the legalisation debate has a higher profile than for many years. Increased drug use by younger people and the connection with acquisitive and, recently, violent crime, have helped broaden the debate beyond cannabis. Legalising drugs such as heroin and cocaine has become a hot media topic as commentators speculate that spread of HIV, crime and other social ills could be reduced at a stroke of the legislator's pen. Last October the intervention of the Law Lord, Lord Woolf, and the drug-related murder of a police officer in London, helped stimulate a fresh rash of comment. Here are some of the highlights from just a single month of the debate.

THE DISTINGUISHED JOURNALIST

"I ... have been forced to the conclusion that our present drug laws cause far more crime than they prevent, including ... assault and murder ...[They] might have been written to enrich the mafia ... All drugs should be sold through licensed outlets ... They should be taxed ... but ... not so expensive as to make smuggling profitable ... This should apply to hard as well as soft drugs ..."

Lord Rees-Mogg, *former editor of the* Times *and until recently chair of the Broadcasting Standards Council, writing in the* Daily Mail, *30 October 1993.*

THE TOP HOME OFFICE ANALYST

"Would you decriminalise drugs?"
"Oh, without a doubt ... in America they don't even process crime ... They're so overwhelmed by it ... That's because they're so stupid about drugs ... [their] inner cities are totally destroyed and handed over to criminals, all to protect the price of crack and heroin."

Mary Tuck, *former head of research at the Home Office involved with criminal statistics, interviewed by David Hare in the* Independent on Sunday, *10 October 1993.*

THE MPS

"What should worry people most is the criminal activity associated with the supply of drugs. Legalisation of cannabis would eliminate much [of this]. Decriminalisation of all drugs would enable other health issues such as adulteration and needle infection to be addressed ... we need a Royal Commission to review current legislation ..."

Tony Banks, *Labour MP for Newham North West, writing in* Tribune, *15 October 1993.*

"Liberal Democrats should take a 'relaxed' view of the legalisation of cannabis ... Is it not true that the young people who purchase cannabis in the street buy it from the very people who will also supply them with crack, cocaine and all the other hard drugs?"

Angela Browning, *Liberal Democrat MP, in a Commons debate on crime, 28 October 1993.*

"If we legalise cannabis, we will just whet the appetites of children for more and more hard drugs, and create more crime."

Sir Ivan Lawrence, *Conservative MP, in a Commons debate on crime, 28 October 1993.*

"It now seems to be fashionable and politically correct to call for the decriminalisation of cannabis, but I would be very sorry if this ... paved the way for a freer availability and a new drug culture."

David Alton, *Liberal MP and vice-chair of the All Party Parliamentary Drugs Misuse Group,* Liverpool Echo, *20 October 1993.*

THE JUDGES

"Should we not at least consider whether it would be preferable for drugs, or at least some drugs, to be lawfully available in controlled circumstances, so that it would no longer be necessary for addicts to commit crimes to feed their addiction?"

Lord Woolf, *Law Lord and former Lord Justice of Appeal, speaking in London on 12 October 1993.*

"The creation of an underground criminal world – the drug culture – outweighs the evils of legalising drugs. The enormous amount of money saved [by legalising] could be spent on educational programmes."

A **serving judge** *from London in a call to BBC Radio's* Crimewatch *programme, 19 October 1993.*

THE POLICE OFFICERS

"If this is a war on drugs, then we are losing ... Policing efforts ... may not only be failing, but contributing to the problem ... It may be time to consider an alternative ... I am not suggesting legalisation as a way of abandoning the war. I want to win."

Eddie Ellison, *recently retired Metropolitan Police detective chief superintendent,* Police Review, *15 October 1993.*

"Even if, heaven forbid, the authorities sold and taxed drugs, organised crime would undercut the price, intimi-date and distort the market, while still controlling production ... It is too soon to say we have failed ... There is no place at this crucial time for faint-hearted revisionists."

Graham Saltmarsh *of the National Criminal Intelligence Service,* Police Review, *22 October 1993.*

"While politicians wring their hands ... as drug-related crime escalates and police officers face increasing danger from armed criminals, they would do well to reflect whether the very laws they swear to strengthen are the cause of the problem they seek to address ... As Margaret Thatcher said, you cannot buck the market."

Gordon Payne *of the Hampshire Constabulary,* Police Review, *22 October 1993.*

THE NATIONAL PAPERS

"Let's legalise cannabis, says Labour MP Tony Banks, and the problem will go away ... Some hope! It would simply focus [the gangsters'] minds on harder drugs."
News of the World *leader, 24 October 1993.*

"Crude decriminalisation will not work ... Something more subtle is needed ... and is already in operation in Holland ... Soft drugs ... are decriminalised through prosecution policy ... Hard drugs should not be legalised, but we should review the old British idea of making them available to addicts on prescription."
Guardian *leader, 14 October 1993.*

"If the money stops, so will murder ... The transfer of profits from the [drug] dealers to the state by some form of licensed, decriminalised sale ... would shift the burden from the police to the NHS ... not even to debate the effect of such a change shows a collective lack of nerve among this country's politicians."
Independent *leader, 23 October 1993, after the drug-related murder of a London police officer.*

"There are good reasons for thinking that drugs should be made legal ... The campaign for a debate on drug legalisation has greater weight now that one of the most respected and humane figures of the legal establishment is one of its public advocates."
Independent *leader, 13 October 1993, reacting to Lord Woolf's speech (see* The Judges*).*

Existing drugs strategy across the UK

Introduction

The Government's existing strategy for tackling drug misuse has been in place since the mid-1980s. The UK-wide strategy was described in detail in *UK Action on Drug Misuse: The Government's Strategy*, published in 1990, but in 1994 and 1995, each of the individual nations in the UK published their own strategies for action on drug misuse over the next three years.

In 1994 the Government published a Green paper called *Tackling Drugs Together*, outlining the strategy for England for 1995-1998. This paper stimulated an extensive public debate. Conferences and seminars were held around the country, and the Green paper discussed in both Houses of Parliament. By the end of the consultation period, over four hundred individuals and organisations had made their views and suggestions known, and the Government made account of responses when revising the strategy.

The strategy involves simultaneous action on five main fronts:

• Improving international co-ordination to reduce supplies from abroad
• Increasing the effectiveness of police and customs enforcement
• Maintaining effective deterrents and tight domestic controls
• Developing prevention publicity, education and community action
• Improving treatment and rehabilitation

The emphasis is on multi-agency co-ordination both at national and local levels, in order to make progress toward these aims.

---

adapted from *Tackling Drugs Together*, HMSO 1994 and 1995 (Government Green Paper and White Paper).

Scotland's strategy is ahead of that in all the other countries. A Ministerial Drug Task Force, established by the Secretary of State, reviewed the Scottish position. Its report, *Drugs in Scotland: Meeting the Challenge*, published in October 1994, set out a comprehensive strategy for action and identified the roles that statutory and non-statutory agencies can play both in preventing drug misuse and in providing services for misusers. The task force recommendations, which placed particular emphasis on a co-ordinated, multi-sectoral approach involving local communities, are being implemented. The national co-ordinating committee is the Scottish Advisory Committee on Drugs.

The Welsh Office is establishing a Welsh Drug and Alcohol Unit, which will form partnerships with other Welsh national organisations to oversee activity to combat drugs and alcohol misuse. A Welsh strategy is being developed.

Northern Ireland's Committee on drug misuse published their draft drug misuse policy in March 1995. The consultation period ended on May 31, and recommendations are being made to the Northern Ireland Department of Health and Social Services. The draft strategy is modelled closely on the English one, but since the population is smaller, and services more integrated, local drug action teams are not proposed as a basis for co-ordination, a role played for the province as a whole by the Committee on Drug Misuse.

Responsibility for the strategy in England is shared by several Departments and Agencies, including the Home Office, the Department of Health, the Department for Education, HM Customs and Excise, HM Prison Services, the Foreign and Commonwealth Office and the Overseas Development Administration. In Scotland, the Scottish Office coordinates policy across the range of health, education, police, prison and social work services in tackling drug misuse. The Welsh Office and the Northern Ireland Office are responsible for health and education policies in Wales and Northern Ireland respectively. Independent advice to the Government on drugs issues is provided by the Advisory Council on the Misuse of Drugs.

The Advisory Council on the Misuse of Drugs

The Advisory Council on the Misuse of Drugs (ACMD) was established under *the Misuse of Drugs Act 1971*. Its terms of reference, as set out by the 1971 Act, are:

• "to keep under review the situation in the United Kingdom with respect to drugs which are going or appear to them likely to be misused and of which the misuse is having or appears to them capable of having harmful effects sufficient to constitute a social problem"; and

• to advise Ministers on measures to be taken.

ACMD currently has 36 members comprising academic experts and professional practitioners in the area of drug misuse.

The bulk of ACMD's work is carried out by its committees and working groups. At present, these cover AIDS/HIV, hepatitis, the criminal justice system, prevention, information (including research and statistics) and legislation.

ACMD publishes reports on aspects of the drugs problem. Recent reports have covered AIDS, drug education in schools, the role of the probation services and criminal justice community resources. Such reports are highly respected for their authority and play an important part in developing Government policy.

International cooperation

The main elements in the UK's strategy for dealing with international drug matters are through bilateral representations and multilateral action. The UK aims to take action to reinforce and invigorate the fight against international drug trafficking. The UK will use its unique position in the UN, European Union and Commonwealth to promote a coherent approach across the three organisations.

United Nations

The UK fully supports the leadership role of the United Nations International Drug Control Programme (UNDCP), formed in 1991 as the focal point in the UN for coordinating international assistance and action against drugs.

The UK is also an active member of the Dublin Group, which brings together European Union and other donor countries to coordinate policies and assistance towards transit and producer countries. Several initiatives have been taken through local Dublin Groups to seek a greater commitment from governments in both transit and producer countries to tackle the illegal drug trade and introduce appropriate legislation.

The UK attaches particular importance to the 1988 UN Drugs Convention which provides a comprehensive framework for international cooperation against drug trafficking. The UK ratified the Convention in June 1991 and is extending it to UK Dependent Territories.

Europe

Within the European Union, prior to the Treaty on European Union ("the Maastricht Treaty") coming into force, the UK was closely involved in a number of fora, including the European Committee to Combat Drugs, which dealt with drugs issues within Member States, and the European Political Cooperation Drugs Working Group, which dealt with matters outside Europe.

Title VI of the Maastricht Treaty aims to enhance cooperation between governments in tackling drug misuse. Such cooperation will take place in the judicial, customs and police areas and includes the establishment of a European Police Office (EUROPOL) for exchanging information. The first phase of EUROPOL has involved the establishment of a Drugs Unit (EDU), concerned with intelligence on illegal drug trafficking and associated money laundering. Article 129 (the "Public Health" chapter) of the Maastricht Treaty also encourages community action on prevention of major health scourges, including drug dependence. This should lead to increase exchanges of experience and information between European Union countries on preventing drug misuse, as well as further collaboration such as European Drug Prevention Week.

At the European Union Heads of Government Summit in Corfu in June 1994, the Prime Minister proposed an action plan to tackle drug trafficking and other organised crime. This plan involved intelligence gathering, strengthening the drugs work of EUROPOL, domestic action, and the sharing of national expertise, both within the European Union and with Central Eastern Europe.

The UK is also involved in the Council of Europe's "Pompidou Group", which is the primary forum for developing wider cooperation on drugs matters in Europe. The UK chaired the Group from 1984 to 1990 and has more recently encouraged participation in the Group by former Iron Curtain countries. The UK has ratified the Council of Europe Anti-Doping Convention which concerns the elimination of drug misuse in sport.

Assistance to other countries

The UK continues to help other countries no only to curb the production, trafficking and consumption of drugs but also to tackle their own domestic drugs problems. UK overseas drugs-related assistance in 1992-93 amounted to some £12 million. UK multilateral assistance is mainly channelled through UNDCP and has included support for major projects in Bolivia (rural development), Pakistan (crop substitution) and Afghanistan (supply reduction). The UK has also supported UNDCP projects on law enforcement in the countries of the former Soviet Union, Greece, the Baltic States, Turkey, Lebanon and Uganda, on legislation in the Baltic Statesand on demand reduction in Jamaica. UK bilateral assistance has focused mainly on the Andean countries (including £12.4 million of training and equipment for Colombia since 1989), the Caribbean, Central and South Eastern Europe, Africa and the Golden Crescent and the Golden Triangle areas of South West and South East Asia.

The continued threat of the Balkan Route for the trafficking of opiates from South-West Asia to Europe remains a particular focus of UK drugs-related assistance, which has taken the form of equipment, training and advice aimed at improving controls in the region on the illegal movement of drugs. For example, in 1992 the UK provided a drugs intelligence computer system for the Czech authorities ("Project Charles").

Customs and police work closely with foreign law enforcement agencies both in the conduct of operations and the exchange of intelligence. The intelligence effort is supported by Drugs Liaison Officers based in British Embassies in drug producer and transit countries. In-country drug law enforcement training is a significant element in UK bilateral assistance. Since 1990, HM Customs and Excise have trained over 2000 overseas law enforcement officers in some 50 countries. The Overseas Development Administration also funds training for overseas Customs and Excise officials, police and drug enforcement groups through its aid programme.

In recent years, growing attention has been paid internationally to the need to address demand for drugs as well as supply as part of an integrated approach to tackling drug misuse. Department of Health officials work closely with colleagues in the Home Office on initiatives from the UN, the Council of Europe Pompidou Group and the European Union to ensure the UK makes a full contribution to effective international responses and shares the expertise which it is widely recognised exists in the UK. The Department of Health is involved with initiatives within the Council of Europe Pompidou Group to provide training and examples of good practice on demand reduction particularly aimed at cooperation with Eastern and Central Europe. Department of Health officials are also members of the Management Board of the new European Monitoring Centre for Drugs and Drug Addiction which, in cooperation with other relevant international bodies, will be working to improve information on drugs and drug addiction, concentrating in the first three years on the reduction of demand for drugs.

Enforcement action

HM Customs and Excise and the police services have responsibility for enforcing anti-drugs legislation. To ensure a clear understanding of the respective role of each agency, the Home Office has published guidelines that remain part of the Government's strategy:

> "HM Customs and Excise have primary responsibility for preventing and detecting the illegal import and export of controlled drugs, the investigation of organisations and individuals engaged in international drugs smuggling, their prosecution and the identification of any proceeds of such crime"

> "The police have a particular responsibility for dealing with offences of manufacture, supply and possession of drugs."

Inevitably, there is overlap between the two agencies both in drugs operational activity and in intelligence gathering. Most major cases, save those concerned exclusively with UK-based manufacture, involve elements of joint working. Many Customs cases arise from police information and Customs pass information to the police where the offence is clearly one of possession or supply. The National Criminal Intelligence Service brings together staff from both police and Customs. It collects and collates information relating to current drugs operations and distributes intelligence to both services. NCIS is staffed by police, Customs and civilian personnel and has five regional offices and a dedicated Drugs Division comprising over 100 staff.

HM Customs and Excise

HM Customs and Excise deploy 5,100 staff on drugs work and anti-smuggling, including 800 specialist investigation staff based in London and five regional centres, intelligence staff, lawyers and support staff. There are two principal aspects of Customs' control for drugs: preventive control at ports and airports and through coastal surveillance; and specialist investigations based on information and intelligence gathered from various sources at home and overseas, designed to anticipate and intercept consignments of drugs and to arrest the organisers of smuggling attempts.

Police

Approximately 1,300 police officers are solely engaged in drugs work, while many others have a major commitment. The six Regional Crime Squads in England and Wales alone employ around 345 officers in their dedicated drugs wings, while the Royal Ulster Constabulary's dedicated Drugs Squad comprises over 20 officers. About 80 per cent of the work of the Scottish Crime Squad, which comprises 85 officers, relates to drugs.

Deterrence and domestic controls

The *Misuse of Drugs Act 1971* establishes the controlled status of drugs liable to be misused. The Act and its associated *Misuse of Drugs Regulations* render unlawful the importation and exportation, production, supply and possession of such drugs without authority. The Regulations also provide for the legal production and distribution of controlled drugs for pharmaceutical purposes and impose requirements in respect of prescription, record keeping and the destruction of drugs. The strictest controls are applied to those drugs with little or no acknowledged medical use.

The Government aims to deter drug traffickers and dealers by providing high maximum penalties and by depriving them of the proceeds of their crimes. These deterrent effects have been strengthened in recent years by:

- The *Criminal Justice (International Cooperation) Act 1990*, which makes it an offence to manufacture certain substances which knowingly would be used in the unlawful production of a controlled drug.

- The *Criminal Justice Act 1993*, which substantially strengthened the existing powers for confiscating the proceeds of all types of crime including drug trafficking. The drugs provisions have recently been consolidated in the Drug Trafficking Act 1994, including the power to forfeit drug trafficking money which is being imported into or exported from the UK.

In 1992, the UK was the first country to ratify the 1990 Council of Europe Convention on Laundering, Search, Seizure and Confiscation of the Proceeds from Crime, which contains detailed provision for multilateral cooperation in confiscating the proceeds of drug trafficking and other serious crime. In addition, the UK has concluded 30 full bilateral confiscation agreements and arrangements, and plays a major role in the G7 Financial Action Task Force established in 1989 in response to the threat of drug money laundering.

In terms of sentencing, the framework introduced by the *Criminal Justice Act 1991* requires that sentences passed by the courts should be commensurate with the seriousness of the offence committed by the offender. Where a court considers that an offence is not so serious that only a custodial penalty is justified but is serious enough to merit a community sentence, the court must ensure that the order or orders it makes are the most suitable for the offender, and in doing so may take into account any information about the offender which is before it. Attendance at programmes to deal with dependency may be included in a probation order (or the probation element of a combination order) either voluntarily, as part of supervision under the order, or as a mandatory requirement of the order. The Home Secretary has published a consultation document on proposals to replace the current array of community sentences with a new integrated community sentence. This consultation provides an opportunity to review the court's powers to consider the part that treatment for drug misuse could play in the rehabilitation of offenders serving a community sentence.

The Prison Service in England and Wales has included reducing the level of drug misuse in prisons as one of ten strategic priorities in its 1994-97 Corporate Plan. The new prison service drugs strategy will further commit the Service to vigorous measures against drug dealing and the misuse of drugs, including mandatory drug testing, as well as to the provision of effective support for drug misusers.

The *Criminal Justice and Public Order Act 1994* introduced powers for prison officers to require prisoners to provide a sample of urine for drug testing purposes. In parallel amendments to Prison and Young Offender Institution Rules in England and Wales introduced a new offence in these establishments of unauthorised administration of a controlled drug. The new rule is to be policed by a widespread drug testing programme and acts as both a deterrent to those who wish to misuse drugs within prison, and as a means of identifying those who may need assistance with drug problems.

Prevention and education

The Government aims to discourage people, particularly young people, from ever misusing drugs. The principal prevention activities in the existing strategy are:

• education;
• prevention activity undertaken in local communities by Home Office Drugs Prevention Initiative teams, the health service and voluntary organisations; and
• national information and publicity campaigns, including European Drug PreventionWeek.

Education

Aspects of education about drugs feature both in the mandatory National Curriculum in England and Wales and in the wider curriculum offered by schools. Schools are encouraged to set education about drugs in the context of programmes of preventive health education which give pupils the facts, which emphasise the benefits of a healthy lifestyle and help young people to make informed and responsible choices. Many schools have made use of the curriculum guidance on health education issued in 1990 by the former National Curriculum Council to develop their programmes of drug and health education.

Within National Curriculum science, pupils learn about the harmful effects of the misuse of drugs. The message is reinforced by returning to this study at various stages during compulsory schooling. The content of the National Curriculum is currently under review with a view to slimming down individual subjects. References to drug education have been retained, reflecting the importance the Government gives to preventive drug education. Under the published consultation proposals for National Curriculum science, as they move through school, pupils will continue to be taught about the harmful effects of the misuse of drugs.

Between 1986 and 1993, the Department for Education supported £33 million of local education authority expenditure in the field of drug and health education, mostly used to put in place local drug and health education coordinators. Schools continue to make use of the advice, information, training, curriculum development and other support provided by drug and health education coordinators. During European Drug Prevention Week 1992, the Department for Education and the Welsh Office issued *Drug Misuse and the Young* containing guidance for teachers, lecturers and youth workers.

In Scotland, education about drugs is taught as one element of health education which is offered in all schools. The school curriculum in Scotland is not laid down by Parliament and responsibility lies with education authorities and head teachers to decide the broad scope and detailed content of study programmes. A range of teaching materials is available to schools but the main teaching package on drug education is *Drugwise Too*, aimed at 10 to 14 year olds. This was distributed to all Scottish schools at the end of 1992. In addition, the Health Education Board for Scotland produces important materials for public education and for use by professionals, including teachers.

In Northern Ireland schools, health education is a compulsory element of the curriculum for all pupils up to 16. Health programmes include, at appropriate stages, education on drugs in the context of social and personal development.

The Department for Education annually supports a range of bodies and projects in the field of preventive drug education. In 1994, one example is participation in the European Network of Health Promoting Schools which will help to identify and promote effective preventive drug education policy and practice both in the curriculum and in relation to drug-related incidents on school premises.

Youth services agencies and individual youth workers offer education programmes and individual counselling and support that can make an important contribution to tackling drugmisuse. The Department for Education has funded research, materials' production and project work. The Department also funds the National Youth Agency , a body with a wide-ranging youth service remit including training, curriculum development and dissemination. Its practical training guide *Health Education in Youth Work* contains details of drug misuse teaching resources.

Further and higher education institutions also contribute to the effort to tackle drug misuse. As independent, autonomous bodies, they individually adopt rules governing the prohibition of drugs from college premises and disciplinary sanctions. They provide welfare and counselling services for their students.

Community action

The Home Office Drugs Prevention Initiative has, since its launch in 1990, promoted the prevention of drug misuse both nationally and locally. The task is to mobilise local communities to promote and sustain drug prevention activity, and is carried out by 20 locally based teams in England, Scotland and Wales, supported by a central unit in London. These teams advise and work with local people, businesses, churches, local media and voluntary organisations. The approaches to drug prevention which have been adopted include raising drug awareness; education and training; diversionary activities; supporting community development; and working with criminal justice agencies. Since 1990, the Drugs

Prevention Initiative have financially supported over 1,500 specific projects, as well as contributing to the development and coordination of local drug prevention strategies. Funding for the Drugs Prevention Initiative has been renewed for a further four years from 1 April 1995. Twelve larger regional Drugs Prevention Teams have been set up, building from the existing teams in England.

All projects supported by the Drugs Prevention Initiative are evaluated, often by independent bodies such as universities and external research organisations. The Drugs Prevention Initiative is collating evidence of the key lessons learned, both on good practice and pitfalls, to assist future preventive work. One of the key findings of recent research, commissioned by the Drugs Prevention Initiative, into the public's views on drug misuse has revealed a great deal of support for the involvement of the community in action against drugs.

Health Authorities are responsible for ensuring that their local populations receive appropriate health education and promotion programmes. Their activities include the distribution of publicity material (posters and leaflets), teaching packs and videos about the dangers of drug misuse. They work closely with local authorities, education authorities, Drugs Prevention Initiative teams, probation services, schools and voluntary services. Health promotion initiatives are aimed at both drug misusers in touch with services and those who are not. Many service providers have created outreach services which are aimed at hard-to-reach populations. Outreach work aims to encourage individuals to contact services and to help influence behaviour away from high-risk activities such as needle sharing and unsafe sex.

National information campaigns

Since the mid 1980s, the Government has run several major health education and information campaigns about drug misuse, aimed at various target groups including young people. In 1991-92 the Government launched two major campaigns which focused on the role of parents in preventing drug and solvent misuse. National press and television publicity promoted published guides for parents, while regional campaigns in England and Wales highlighted local services.

During its Presidency of the European Community, the UK hosted an international two-day event for European Drug Prevention Week 1992 organised by the Department of Health. A media seminar on the first day aimed to stimulate the interest of the European media in thinking about their role in drug prevention and to raise the profile of prevention among an audience of opinion formers from the fields of health, education, the criminal justice system, Government and business. A conference for professionals organised around 18 inter-disciplinary workshops enabled European drug prevention professionals to exchange information and ideas about developing drug prevention strategies. A report on the professionals' conference was published in 1994. During the week the Department of Health launched a video package for parents, *Drugs – A Family Matter* which aimed to inform parents about the problem of drug and solvent misuse, and provided factual information to help them to talk to their children.

Following the success of its 1991-92 competition for schools, *Acting Against Drug Misuse*, the Government has run a second competition for schools in 1993-94, *Acting for Health – Drugs, Smoking and Alcohol Misuse* which aims to encourage young people to think about the consequences of substance misuse. The competition invited schools to submit storyboards on substance misuse issues which could be made into a video or short film.

In January 1994, the Government launched a new television and press campaign aimed at parents. The key message was how important it was for parents to discuss drugs with their children. To this end, a leaflet *Drugs and Solvents – You and Your Child* was produced. The leaflet was translated into ten ethnic languages and produced in large print and audio cassette versions. A British Sign Language video was also produced. The campaign also included the production of an information leaflet for 13 to 18 year olds and an updated version of a leaflet for 8 to 12 year olds.

Independent evaluation of national information campaigns has shown that they have raised awareness of drug issues. For example, research into the *Drugs – A Family Matter* video package showed that it had generated considerable interest, was very likely to be used, and was seen as being of great benefit in helping parents and others to preempt serious drug and solvent misuse by young people. An evaluation of the parents' campaign showed that 95 per cent of parents believe they have a responsibility to talk to their children about the dangers of drugs and solvents, and 87 per cent believe they have the primary responsibility to do so.

In England, a national conference for parents on drug prevention organised by the Department of Health was held in June 1994. This provided a positive message to parents about the key role they can play in preventing their children from misusing drugs, responding to their need for information while also looking at parenting skills and communication. Initial feedback shows that the conference was well received by those who attended and likely to be of real help to them in their work with other parents.

European Drug Prevention Week 1994

The second European Drug Prevention Week took place between 15-22 October 1994. The theme was drug prevention and the young, and the primary target audience, 8-21 year olds. Parents and professionals who work with young people were a further target. The objectives of the week were to raise awareness and increase knowledge about drugs and their effects, to facilitate coordinated action at local level, and to encourage young people concerned about drugs to seek help. The response was good, with over 6,000 calls to the special drugs helpline, over half of which were from young people under 18 years of age.

The national event in England is the award ceremony for the schools competition on substance misuse *Acting for Health*. In Scotland, a series of events is addressing the issues of drug misuse and the family, and drug misuse in rural areas. A representative group of young people will debate drug prevention issues. A sixth-form peer led conference, *Young People Taking the Lead*, and a second peer education conference for young people and support workers are taking place in Wales. Two cross-border initiatives and a multi-agency conference in Belfast, *Addressing Drug Misuse: Issues and Approaches*, are being planned in Northern Ireland.

National publicity campaigns during European Drug Prevention Week include a youth radio campaign on local FM stations and a re-run of the television campaign targeting parents. A telephone helpline is provided as part of the radio campaign, offering access to free literature and advice. Further collaboration with the media includes the BBC Radio 1 social action programme, *Drug Alert*, Channel 4 schools programmes, and the youth, regional and national press. Coverage on regional, national and satellite television is encouraged by the distribution of a video news release.

Community Safety and Crime Prevention

In addition to crime prevention measures specifically targeted on drug-related crime, more general initiatives can also have an impact. One example is the Safer Cities programme (now part of the Single Regeneration Budget) which aims to reduce crime generally and in doing so has supported many projects with drug-related components.

The Home Office and the Department of the Environment issue planning guidance and practical design advice to help produce attractive, well managed environments that help to discourage criminal behaviour of all kinds and reduce opportunities for crime. This includes advice on the design and layout of new housing developments and on changes to the form and management of existing housing estates, land uses that keep town centres lively and well-used, use of street furniture to prevent crimes like ram-raiding, and installation of CCTV systems.

Treatment and rehabilitation

Health care services

The aim is to provide a comprehensive range and choice of local services to help drug misusers give up drugs and maintain abstinence. Services also promote better health and reduce the risks of drug misuse, including infections associated with sharing injecting equipment such as HIV and hepatitis. Services include residential detoxification and rehabilitation, community drug dependency services, needle and syringe exchange schemes, advice and counselling, and after-care and support services. Facilities are provided by both statutory and independent agencies.

Since 1986, the Department of Health has earmarked additional funding through health authorities for the expansion of services for drug misusers in England. The Department's total contribution has grown from £15.5 million in 1990-91 to over £25 million in 1994-95. The Department is also providing almost £700, 000 in 1994-95 as grant-aid to national voluntary organisations concerned with drug misuse.

The Scottish Office makes available additional resources each year to Health Boards in support of services for the treatment and rehabilitation of drug misusers. Since 1986, these allocations have amounted to some £17 million and in 1994-95 nearly £2.6 million has been made available. The Scottish Office also provides grant assistance to Scottish national voluntary organisations concerned with drug misuse.

Since 1985, the Welsh Office has provided resources on a recurrent basis to facilitate the development of drug prevention and treatment and rehabilitation services. In 1993-94, over £2.5 million was made available to statutory and voluntary projects to combat drug misuse.

In Northern Ireland, the Department of Health and Social Services allocation to the four Health and Social Services Boards includes expenditure on treatment and rehabilitation services for drug misusers. Over £100,000 was spent in 1993-94 and this included a grant to Northlands, a voluntary organisation providing regional services in the area of substance misuse.

General practitioners are encouraged to address the needs of drug misusers. Guidelines on clinical management, *Drug Misuse and Dependence*, were issued to all doctors in 1991. The exact treatment offered varies from case to case and depends on the clinical judgment of the doctor concerned.

In April 1994, the Minister of Health announced a wide-ranging review of treatment services for drug misusers in England (the Effectiveness Review). The aim is to determine how effective such services are in helping people to stop taking drugs and in reducing drug misuse and the damage associated with it. The review is being conducted by a Task Force from a broad range of backgrounds, chaired by the Reverend Dr John Polkinghorne, and a report is due in 1996.

Community Care services

In addition to health care services, the Government attaches a high priority to the establishment of effective community-based care services for drug misusers and their families. In April 1993, local authorities throughout the UK took over responsibility from the Department of Social Security for assessing the community care needs of client groups, including drug misusers, and for purchasing services with resources transferred from the Department of Social Security.

Since April 1991, there has also been a specific grant payable to local authorities in England which enables them to support voluntary organisations providing services to drug and alcohol misusers. A total of £8.2 million has been provided since 1991-92 of which £2.4 million alone has been allocated for 1994-95. Since the grant's inception, the emphasis has changed from residential care to new community-based alternatives. From 1994-95, all new applications will be assessed on the principle of "outcome funding" which involves services providers identifying clear results and setting targets against which to measure progress.

Improving information about drug misuse

Under the *Misuse of Drugs Act 1971*, doctors are required to notify the Chief Medical Officer at the Home Office of patients whom they consider to be addicted to heroin, cocaine or other opiate-type controlled drugs. Data supplied to the Home Office is analysed and published as an annual statistical bulletin. The most recent bulletin, *Statistics of Drug Addicts notified to the Home Office, United Kingdom, 1993*, was published in June 1994. This information also enables a doctor to check whether a notifiable drug misuser is seeking simultaneous treatment from morethan one doctor.

Following the issue of guidance in 1989, regional health authorities in England have set up databases of drug misusers who present themselves to local agencies for treatment, either for the first time or after an interval of more than six months. Scotland and Wales have established similar databases. These databases aim to enable health authorities to target the development of services to meet changing needs and to monitor the current use of services.

To provide a clearer picture of patterns of drug misuse among the population at large, the use of social surveys is being developed by the Home Office and other Government Departments. Two initial surveys of this kind were the 'Four Cities' survey and the contemporaneous self-report element of the *1992 British Crime Survey*.

A new European Monitoring Centre for Drugs and Drug Addiction has been established to provide 'objective, reliable and comparable information at European level concerning drugs, drug addiction and their consequences'. It has considerable resources at its disposal. (5.35 million ECU in 1995).

Communicable diseases and drug misuse

Injecting drug misusers are a major risk group for infection with blood-borne viruses such as HIV, hepatitis B and hepatitis C. One of the targets in the Government's strategy for health in England set out in Health of the Nation, is to reduce the percentage of injecting drug misusers who report that they share needles from 20 per cent in 1990 to 10 per cent by 1997 and 5 per cent by 2000. A handbook on the action that health authorities could take to achieve this target was published in January 1993.

More than 300 needle and syringe exchange schemes have been set up since the mid-1980s. These schemes recognise that, while abstinence remains the ultimate aim, steps must be taken to reduce the spread of blood-borne viruses by drug misusers who are not yet willing to give up injecting. Specific funding totalling nearly £7 million has been made available since 1992-93 for the development of needle exchange schemes in pharmacies which provide sterile equipment and disposal facilities. Advice is provided both on drug misuse problems and the risk of acquiring and transmitting HIV and other infections. General practitioners may also issue injecting equipment to drug misusers. It is likely that the reduction in the number of diagnoses of HIV infections has been helped by the development of needle exchange schemes as well as programmes of prevention and education targeted at injecting drug misusers.

Public expenditure

It is estimated that the Government spent about £526 million in 1993-94 on tackling drug misuse across the UK. This breaks down as below:

- Police/Customs enforcement   *£209 million*
- Deterrence/controls   *£137 million*
- Prevention/education   *£104 million*
- Treatment/rehabilitation   *£61 million*
- International action   *£15 million*

The direct cost of tackling drug misuse is also borne by many private organisations such as businesses, charities and the voluntary sector generally.

What help is available for drug users and does it work?

by Ross Coomber

Introduction

There are a broad range of services and treatments available for those dependent on drugs. This chapter will outline the main types of services available, the treatment options that can be found within them and provide an insight into how successful these treatments are for the individual drug user and also, on a more general level, for society. This chapter will mainly deal with heroin dependency because in the UK heroin is the main illicit drug on which people become dependent and that treatment services are best equipped to deal with.

Types of treatment

Street agencies

These are locally-based agencies offering a range of services which might include a telephone helpline, drop-in centre, home visits and outreach (where drug workers go into the community to 'reach' drug users). As well as information and advice (on the whole range of drugs), street agencies often provide individual and group counselling and other support services for those with drug problems and for those who are becoming, or who have become, abstinent from drugs. Many street agencies work closely with GPs either to provide primary health care and/or to provide prescriptions for withdrawal, detoxification and occasionally stabilisation through maintenance prescribing (see Treatment options below). Harm reduction services such as the provision of free condoms and safer sex advice/information, as well as needle/syringe exchanges and information and advice on safer injecting practices are also within their remit.

Drug Dependency Units (DDUs)

Whereas the street agencies are nearly all in the voluntary (non-statutory) sector, DDUs are all part of National Health Service provision, and as such are often found in hospitals, as opposed to 'in the community'. They have a variety of services mirroring many of those provided by the street agency, and they also provide various 'clinical' treatments such as detoxification through medium and short-term prescribing. Most will provide longer-term prescribing (mainly opiates) for stabilising those for whom it is deemed appropriate. Maintenance prescribing is not normally offered and some do not offer a prescription service at all. As might be expected in a clinical setting, psychiatric and psychological treatment is also available. Inpatient as well as outpatient detoxification may be available.

Community drug teams

The 'community arm' of statutory provision. Services provided are similar to those offered by the street agencies although a drop-in service may not be available. They may have closer links with the DDU and as such access to clinical treatments (including psychiatric and psychological) through referral and liaison.

Residential services

These services provide accommodation, food and support in order to help the user become drug-free. Often they are located in areas well away from the temptations of inner city life. Most of these services require the client to be drug-free when entering the programme and be prepared to become a committed part of a hierarchical community structure within which they learn to deal with a drug-free lifestyle through various individual and group support mechanisms. The different residential services are often based upon particular philosophies relating to drug addiction and what an individual must do to overcome it. Some of them, for example, are based on religious groups.

Self-help groups

Groups such as Narcotics Anonymous (NA) and Families Anonymous are two high profile self-help groups based on the ideas of Alcoholics Anonymous, which essentially sees addiction as a lifelong disease from which there is never a complete 'cure', therefore the only way is total abstinence from any drugs or alcohol.

Narcotics Anonymous involves attendance at meetings, getting and providing mutual support from/to other members and adhering to the '12 Steps' towards a drug-free life. The encouragement to engage with a 'power greater than ourselves' is explicit in the 12 steps to be practised. Formal religious adherence is not the necessary focus of these groups but may nonetheless figure strongly. Families Anonymous seeks to help 'dysfunctional' families recognise the problems which may be inherent in their functioning and which contribute to the addict family member continuing with their addiction, and to provide a 12 Step programme for recovery.

There are other types of family and self-help groups offering advice, support and counselling many of which operate from drug services.

General practitioners

Some GPs have a lot of experience of treating drug users whilst others tend to refer them on to drug services. GPs can potentially offer a range of services relating to health problems associated with drug use, and also prescribe certain drugs for withdrawal, detoxification, stabilisation or maintenance. It is however evident from a number of surveys that most GPs consider the management of drug users and their problems as something that they would prefer to avoid (Glanz 1994).

Notification of drug addicts to the Home Office

A common concern for drug users, and one which may keep many from seeking help, is the belief that treatment agencies will report them to the police, social services and other agencies. In fact, since 1968, doctors have only been required to notify the Home Office of those considered to be addicted to particular drugs such as heroin and cocaine, but not to drugs such as amphetamines, barbiturates or benzodiazepines. As such, drug users, as opposed to addicts, seeking help for drug-related problems are not notified. The 'Addicts Index' is primarily used to keep track of addiction and drug-using trends as well as keeping tabs on doctors prescribing habits. The index is almost entirely confidential and information is passed almost exclusively between treating doctors only. Since the mid-1970s the police have had no access to the index except for exceptional cases which are deemed to be in the interest of the addict themselves or public policy (Mott 1994).

What can services do for drug users?

It is commonly believed that once somebody becomes dependent on heroin, all they have to look forward to is a life of crime and degradation followed by an early death. Certainly this is the fate of some heroin users, but many others either conquer their dependency, either with help from treatment services, or indeed by themselves. This can happen when life events such as acquiring work or getting into a steady relationship mean that drugs are no longer the most important thing in that person's life. There is a concept known as 'maturing out' which indicates that many long-term chronic drug users who survive into their 30s just leave their addiction behind without any formal treatment at all. So, how effective is treatment in 'curing' drug dependency?

"There are many treatments for 'addiction', but relatively few have been shown in controlled trials to have any specific therapeutic effect. Indeed some have never been subjected to controlled evaluation." (Brewer 1993)

Brewer is making the point that there has been relatively little evaluation of treatment, and where this has been carried out, there have often been inconclusive verdicts on the benefits. We shall consider these points again later. In the next section we will briefly review what various treatment options do offer the drug addict.

Treatment options

Detoxification

Clinical detoxification is a particular method of treatment which has been likened to a 'revolving door' (Fazey 1989; Newman 1987) where patients undergo detoxification, relapse (into drug use), undergo detoxification, relapse again and so on. This is because addiction is not simply a physical attachment to a drug. Simple detoxification helps the addict to overcome physical withdrawal symptoms and reach a point of drug-free existence but little more. Detoxification alone does little to 'treat' the other aspects of the 'addictive state' which (Orford 1990) has shown includes complex psychological and social, as well as biochemical traits. Just as the process of becoming dependent on drugs is complex and individual, so is the route out of dependency. The revolving door analogy depicts treatment which clearly helps for a while, and clients acknowledge that help by often returning, but it also demonstrates that in many instances it only provides a start. As Gossop (1987: 161) notes, "There are ... different phases of treatment. One obvious distinction is between getting off and staying off [and] ... it is now clear that detoxification alone is ineffective as a means of helping addicts remain drug-free".

Detoxification programmes have an initial treatment objective of getting the addict to a drug-free state, with the hope that they will be able to stay drug-free, but just getting clients to complete treatment has its difficulties. On this basis, inpatient detoxifications as compared to outpatient detoxifications can be quite successful with some programmes managing to successfully withdraw up to 81 per cent (using gradually reducing amounts of oral methadone over a 10 to 28 day period depending on individual circumstances) from opiates (Gossop *et al* 1986).

With longer-term outpatient detoxification (over six months or more) where the primary objective is to achieve complete abstinence by the end of the treatment programme, success rates may differ but are generally less successful. For example Gossop *et al* found that only 17 per cent of outpatient detoxifications in their evaluation successfully completed the programme compared to 81 per cent of inpatients. For both types of programme, relapse to drugtaking often occurs within the first four weeks after treatment has been completed.

The relapse rate widely perceived to accompany detoxification has led to reported staff frustration, staff 'burn-out' and at times disillusionment with the treatment of users by staff (Newman 1987: 116). Relapse to drugtaking however is not necessarily a relapse to addiction or even continued regular use, even though it often is the result. Gossop *et al* (1987) reported that 45 per cent of 77 opiate addicts, after undergoing an inpatient 21-day reducing methadone detoxification programme, were living in the community and drug-free six months later. Detoxification was followed up by appropriately tailored individual and group-based support and aftercare sessions. Although relapse had occurred for some of these, it had not proved to be decisive. Bradley (1989: 76) has argued that the belief that relapse is both common and decisive is perhaps over-estimated by staff at treatment agencies – although depending on the package offered it is probably more true for some treatment agencies than for others.

The importance of good quality support and aftercare services, tailored to the individual needs of the recovering addict, as evidenced by the Gossop study cited above, would appear to be of great significance to the effectiveness of such treatment.

Residential therapeutic communities

For the most part the 'effectiveness' results for residential therapeutic communities have tended to be mixed (Raistrick and Davidson 1985). In general, a review of the effectiveness of therapeutic communities tends to show that the longer a client remains in residence at such programmes the greater the benefits, particularly for those who stay longer than six months (NIDA 1982; Bleiberg *et al* 1994). One significant problem associated with residential therapeutic communities relates to high drop-out rates (Newman 1987). For those who are able to successfully adjust to the regimes, the benefits appear to be real. Unfortunately, for many, the treatment offered is not deemed to be appropriate or helpful. In fact, Thorley (1981: 149), commenting on a group of former residents where "almost 15 per cent were sure that their stay had done them more harm than good", acknowledged that the experience, whilst very positive for some, may, due to the nature of the programmes and the needs of individuals, in fact be problematic for others.

In recent years however, and in response to changing circumstances like HIV/AIDS and some of the criticisms levelled at them, therapeutic communities have tried to adapt their programmes to make them more amenable to a wider population (Toon and Lynch 1994).

Narcotics Anonymous

Narcotics Anonymous is a self-help organisation which is an offshoot of Alcoholics Anonymous. In the USA, these organisations are well ingrained in both the public mind and media representation, as well as those close to its treatment provision, as being particularly successful (Vaillant 1983). The perception however may be misleading, "I and the director ... tried to prove our efficacy... [and found] compelling evidence that the results of our treatment were no better than the natural history of the disease" (Vaillant 1983, cited in Peele 1990). That is, patients undergoing treatment when compared to a group that did not, fared no better. This perhaps surprising outcome has also been found in other studies (Brandsma *et al* 1980; Ditman *et al* 1967). Christo (1994) has suggested that NA appears to be effective over long periods (after five or six years in bringing anxiety and self-esteem to normal levels) but does not compare this group with those from other treatments, nor does he consider the possibility that NA treatment may actually lengthen the amount of time for anxiety and self-esteem to return to normal due to its particular philosophies and practice.

Again, as with most other types of treatment NA often has high drop-out rates. For some addicts it is undoubtedly a saviour, providing them with support, structure and a focus. For others, like many treatments available, it is too restrictive and unhelpful.

Minnesota model

One form of treatment which is based on the traditions of NA is the Minnesota Model (Curson 1991). A short-term residential therapeutic programme (although outpatient facilities are often available) which has made great claims of success for itself (eg, up to 66 per cent rates of 'cure') and one which received a fair amount of public attention in the mid-1980s. Some of these claims come from self-evaluations and are part of a marketing strategy to secure income (Wells 1994). A review of the studies evaluating the effectiveness of these programmes were however found to be both few in number and often methodologically flawed (Cook 1988). Many however accept that this form of treatment, as with other therapeutic communities, does 'work' for those who accept, and are able to work within, the programme's powerful ideology, which takes much of its lead from the 12 steps of NA, although the 'spiritual' component need not embrace formal religion.

The programme has also a strong tailoring towards individual needs and includes use of "a multidisciplinary team that includes doctors, nurses, social workers, counsellors, psychologists etc" (ibid: 193). Attendance at NA meetings is integrated into the programme itself and is continued after residential treatment has ended.

Methadone maintenance

The use of methadone maintenance programmes, where opiate (usually heroin) addicts are provided with prescriptions of (usually oral) methadone continues to be the subject of much heated debate, despite the fact that it is probably the most evaluated of all treatment programmes (Farrell *et al* 1994). Treatment which is explicitly based around maintenance does not have 'cure' rates in the sense we have been discussing them so far. Advocates of methadone maintenance programmes argue that the value of these programmes lays not in the narrow conception of cure defined as abstinence, but in the broader harm they prevent, both to the individual and society. A recent review of the impact of methadone maintenance concludes, "the randomised studies ... show consistent positive results over vastly different cultural contexts (United States, Hong Kong, Sweden, Thailand) and over two decades of research" (Farrell *et al* 1994: 998).

As we might expect the effectiveness of such programmes varies under different conditions and with different approaches. In other words, there are good programmes and not so good ones. A consistent finding is that programmes which do not restrict treatment to low doses, which provide adequate support services such as good quality counselling, where staff-client relationships are good, and where the objective of treatment is maintenance (and importantly, is perceived as such) as opposed to abstinence, have proved most effective.

Methadone maintenance programmes have been found to be effective in reducing drug-related crime; reducing the rates of HIV infection among treatment populations; reducing risky sharing practices, stabilising lifestyles, and reducing the use of street drugs. The benefits of maintenance programmes thus extends beyond the individual client into the community. This dual benefit has recently been acknowledged by the Advisory Council on the Misuse of Drugs and it has recommended that the benefits of the research and its indications of best practice be incorporated into existing programmes. Two recent studies from the US both report that treatment (particularly methadone maintenance programmes) are up to seven times more cost effective than enforcement as a means to controlling the drugs problem (ISDD 1994).

Methadone maintenance programmes, however, are not currently widespread in Britain and whether a clinic offers such treatment is determined by the clinical head of the unit. Such programmes where they exist will tend to use a methadone linctus which is taken orally, rather than the provision of injectable methadone. The provision (or non-provision) of methadone on a maintenance basis is an example where conflict between what health care professionals may believe to be appropriate or valid treatment may conflict significantly with what some drug users would prefer to have, for example to be prescribed the drug of their choice (heroin in preference to methadone) and/or to be prescribed for maintenance purposes as opposed to detoxification.

Counselling and other psychotherapeutic techniques

Basic information and advice apart, counselling and other psychotherapeutic techniques are an important constituent part of many drug treatments. The techniques vary across and even within treatment programmes. They may range from fairly non-confrontational, and non-directional approaches where the counsellor/therapist seeks to help the client to understand and cope with their problems (many of which may be non-drug related) to more directional and/or confrontational techniques. Both individual and group (clients' family and/or other clients) counselling/therapy is often used.

Because counselling and other psychotherapeutic techniques are often integrated into treatment, evaluation of their efficacy is difficult and few evaluations have been carried out. Some particular therapies, for example those designed to prevent relapse, drawing on a cognitive-behavioural approach, appear to show promise for opiate users but as with other techniques there has been little evaluation and its employment has been relatively limited. As Johns (1994: 1556) has stated "The best of psychological interventions will not have much impact if they cannot be delivered to the patient. There is a need for therapists to be trained in these techniques and for treatment services to have ready access to clinical psychologists and counsellors".

What is the best treatment?

As we have seen, what statistics there are regarding treatment are difficult to interpret for a wide range of reasons. Different types of drug users often find some treatments preferable to others. Some treatment agencies may deal with more difficult or more chronic addicts than others. Some treatments may 'select' their clients to a greater extent than others, artificially boosting success statistics. One treatment programme of a similar type, on paper, may differ significantly in important respects in practice. Too few evaluations of most treatments have taken place to provide reliable information similar to that found for methadone maintenance programmes and comparisons have proved difficult not only between treatments but even between programmes of the same type.

In the USA, the National Institute on Drug Abuse concluded that "Comparisons of post-treatment outcomes of clients within each major treatment modality showed no evidence of differential programme effectiveness" (NIDA 1982). The Advisory Council on the Misuse of Drugs (ACMD) said similarly in 1982 that, "It is not possible therefore on the basis of research undertaken so far to demonstrate conclusively that any one approach is more effective than another" (ACMD 1982: 22). Moreover, as there is no such thing as the typical addict or addiction there is no standard treatment which will work in every or even in most cases. In this light Gossop (1987: 161) has strongly argued that treatment provision needs to take account of individual differences and provide treatment which takes into account the relevant problems. Although most programmes may profess to do this, in practice he suggests the individually tailored programme gives way to the 'typical offer' of a "relatively standard package of procedures and all individuals are required to go through the system".

Rather than arguing that any one treatment programme is best at curing drug addicts we can probably say that the best programme is the one which works for the individual and is able to provide the appropriate treatment, support and response at that moment in time when it is needed.

Does treatment make a difference and what is successful treatment?

Raistrick and Davidson (1985) asked the important question 'does treatment work?' The question was deemed to be worth asking because although we can see that various treatment programmes have a certain amount of success, we also have to recognise that treatment often does not appear to succeed to any greater degree than no treatment. This is, as we said above, is because much drug use, problematic or not, actually ends after an indeterminate period of time.

Information on how many are estimated to leave their addiction behind without recourse to treatment is scarce. In a review of research into non-treatment recovery, Waldorf and Biernacki (1979) found common recovery rates in the populations studied in excess of 50 per cent, some results showed less, some more. There was one famous study of returning Vietnam war veterans which showed that while most of them were using heroin in the war zone, most gave it up when they got home (Robins 1993).

Approximately 20 per cent of enlisted men are considered to have been addicted (predominantly to heroin or opium) whilst serving in Vietnam. One year after their return to the USA a follow-up study showed that 95 per cent of those addicted whilst in Vietnam were no longer addicted. After three years the percentage was 88 per cent and of the 12 per cent who had become re-addicted at some point in the three years, that re-addiction had normally been relatively short-lived (Robins 1993). Treatment cannot explain this incredibly high recovery rate. Only a small percentage received any treatment and of those who did enter treatment on return, their relapse rates, approximately two-thirds, compared poorly to those who did not access treatment.

Raistrick and Davidson (1985) raise the important point that the relationship itself between the treatment provider and the client can have important consequences for treatment effectiveness, citing the case of an experiment involving two groups of 'rapid smokers' as illustrative. One group was given a therapist who carried out the given therapeutic technique coldly and mechanically, giving no support or praise for successes between sessions. This group achieved a success rate (abstinence) of six per cent at follow-up, three months after treatment. This is contrasted to a 73 per cent success rate for the group who had received treatment from a friendly, warm, enthusiastic therapist who provided encouragement for success between sessions. Other studies have found that positive incentives, as opposed to negative ones, tend to incur comparative success in methadone programmes (Strang 1988).

Relationships within treatment generally are far more arbitrary and mixed and as such difficult to assess. What research there is, and it is also true of most treatment settings outside of drug use, suggests that the formation of a positive and encouraging relationship in the right treatment setting can achieve significant impact. This is another indication that treatment can make a difference, but that the technique or programme itself may not always be as important as is often believed.

Oppenheimer *et al* (1990) followed up 116 users new to treatment two and a half years later from three different treatment settings: a drug treatment centre; a therapeutic community, and a crisis intervention centre. The results were impressive, "At follow-up 73 per cent of those currently living in the community were opiate-free. Thirty-seven per cent of the sample were free from all drugs including cannabis at the follow-up" (p.1259). McLellan *et al* (1982) after examining the outcomes of six treatment programmes (different types) and comparing those who had long-term (LT) exposure against those who only had five to 14 days concluded that, "the results from these analyses showed significantly better post-treatment status in virtually all areas for the LT patients" (p.1428). Importantly however, McLellan *et al* were concerned to make the point that although they considered treatment to make a significant and important difference they did not relate their findings to the narrow outcome of 'cure'. Effective outcomes from the methadone maintenance programmes outlined earlier also testify to the fact that treatment does make a significant difference, both to individual and society, even if it does not provide a cure. This raises the important issue of what should be seen as successful treatment.

The question of 'success' is important because not only may drug users have preconceptions about what they need and expect from a service, as may service deliverers what should be provided, but also because funding for services may increasingly come to rely on statistics which demonstrate the effectiveness of any one service. If an expensive drug treatment facility is to be judged in terms of 'cure' alone then many services will be under threat and as we have seen, some programmes do not even have abstinence as their primary aim. So what should be seen as successful treatment? Perhaps a different question could ask 'can drug addicts be successfully helped?'

Harm reduction treatments, such as the provision of new injecting equipment for drug injectors, the teaching of safer injecting behaviour, safer sex advice and provision of free condoms, or the provision of pharmaceutically pure drugs such as methadone amongst others, seeks to reduce the associated harm of drug use. It is not incompatible with curative treatment goals but is not reliant on it. It can be used with drug users not willing to consider stopping drug use with the aim of preventing or reducing harm to individuals and society.

If we accept that different drug users may wish for, or need, different kinds of help at different stages of their addiction or using careers we can acknowledge the potential of harm reduction as appropriate treatment (Todhunter *et al* 1992). Harm reduction as treatment may also enable earlier intervention into a drug-using career because the user is able to make use of treatment earlier. A number of studies (Sheehan *et al* 1986; Hartnoll and Power 1989) have indicated that help-seekers access treatment when they feel they are 'out of control'. Much harm reduction treatment can intervene, with significant effectiveness prior to this moment.

Harm reduction may also mean that treatment starts to reach people that it would never have done otherwise, those who do not access treatment for cure. 'Treatment' in this sense can be seen to be effective, and to make a difference without actually trying to cure.

During the 1980s some drug-using populations had very high levels of HIV infection, acquired predominately through the sharing of infected injecting equipment. Drug users thus represented a significant risk to the general population if they continued to practise unsafe sexual practices with each other and non-drug using partners. The need to reduce risky drugtaking practices (sharing equipment) and risky sexual activity makes the goals of harm reduction as opposed to simple cure for treatment necessary not just for users but for the whole of society.

Conclusion

A review of what happens to drug addicts is far more optimistic than the conventional 'once an addict, always an addict' would have us believe. Large numbers of drug addicts manage to leave their addiction behind either through recourse to the various treatments available or without treatment at all.

What treatment is able to do for any one individual is affected by a range of factors. These include drug user characteristics, the type of programme on offer and the relationship between patients and those providing treatment.

Bibliography

ACMD (1982) *Treatment and Rehabilitation: Report of the Advisory Council on the Misuse of Drugs,* HMSO, London.

Bleiberg, J. L. Croan, J. Briscoe, R. (1994) 'Relationship between treatment length and outcome in a therapeutic community', *The International Journal of the Addictions,* 29 (6) p729-740.

Bradley, B. P. (1989) 'Heroin and the Opiates', *in* Gossop, M. (ed.) (1989) *Relapse and Addictive Behaviour,* Routledge, London.

Brandsma, J. M. Maultsby, M. C. and Welsh, R. J. (1980) *The Outpatient Treatment of Alcoholism,* University Park Press, Baltimore, MD.

Brewer, C. (ed.) (1993) *Treatment Options in Addiction: Medical Management of Alcohol and Opiate Abuse,* Gaskell, London.

Christo, G. and Sutton, S. (1994) 'Anxiety and Self-Esteem as a Function of Abstinence Time Among Recovering Addicts Attending Narcotics Anonymous', *British Journal of Clinical Psychology,* 33, p198-200.

Cook, C. H. (1988) 'The Minnesota Model in the Management of Drug and Alcohol Dependency: miracle, method or myth? Part II. Evidence and Conclusions', *British Journal of Addiction,* 83, p735-748.

Curson, D. A. (1991) 'Private Treatment of Alcohol and Drug Problems in Britain', editorial, *British Journal of Addiction,* 86, p9-11.

Ditman, K. S. (1987) *American Journal of Psychiatry,* 124, p160.

Farrell, M. Ward, J. Mattick, R. *et al.* (1994) 'Methadone maintenance treatment in opiate dependence: a review', *British Medical Journal,* 309, p997-1001.

Fazey, C. J. S. (1989) *What Works? An Evaluation of Drug Treatments for Illicit Drug Users in the United Kingdom and Europe.* Paper presented at the N.D.R.I. What Works? Conference, New York, USA.

Glanz, A. (1994) 'The Fall and Rise of the General Practitioner', *in* Strang, J. and Gossop, M. (1994) *Heroin Addiction and Drug Policy: The British System,* Oxford Medical Publications, Oxford.

Gossop, M. Johns, A. and Green, L. (1986) 'Opiate withdrawal: inpatient versus outpatient programmes and preferred versus random assignation to treatment', *British Medical Journal,* 293, p103-104.

Gossop, M. (1987) 'What is the most effective way to treat opiate addiction?', *British Journal of Hospital Medicine,* September.

Gossop, M. Green, L. Phillips, G. T. Bradley, B. (1987) 'What happens to opiate addicts immediately after treatment: a prospective follow-up study', *British Medical Journal,* 294, p1377-1380.

Hartnoll, R. and Power, R. (1989) 'Why most of Britain's drug users are not looking for help', *Druglink,* March/April, p8-9.

ISDD (1994) 'Major US studies Agree: Treatment Pays for Itself 7 Times Over',*Druglink,* November/December, p8.

Johns, A. (1994) 'Opiate Treatments', *British Journal of Addiction,* 89, p1551-1558.

McLellan, T. Luborsky, L. O'Brien, P. Woody, G. Druley, K. (1982) 'Is Treatment for Substance Abuse Effective?', *Journal of the American Medical Association,* March 12, Volume 247, p1423-1428.

Mott, J. (1994) 'Notification and the Home Office', *in* Strang, J. and Gossop, M. (1994) *Heroin Addiction and Drug Policy: The British System,* Oxford Medical Publications, Oxford.

Newman, R. G. (1987) 'Frustrations Among Professional Working in Drug Treatment Programmes', *British Journal of Addiction,* 82, p115-117.

NIDA (1982) Evaluation of Drug Abuse Treatment Effectiveness – Summary of the DARP Follow-up Research – DHHS No. ADM82-1194.

Oppenheimer, E. Sheehan, M. and Taylor, C. (1988) 'Letting the Client Speak: drug misusers and the process of help seeking', *British Journal of Addiction*, 83, p635-647.

Oppenheimer, E. Sheehan, M. and Taylor, C. (1990) 'What happens to drug misusers? A medium-term follow-up of subjects new to treatment', *British Journal of Addiction*, 85, p1255-1260.

Orford, J. (1990) 'Looking for a synthesis in studying the nature of dependence: facing up to complexity', *in* Edwards, G. and Lader, M. (eds) *The Nature of Drug Dependence*, Oxford Medical Publications, Oxford.

Raistrick, D. and Davidson, R. J. (1985) *Alcoholism and Drug Addiction*, Churchill Livingstone.

Robins, L. (1993) 'Vietnam veterans' rapid recovery from heroin addiction: a fluke or normal expectation?', *Addiction*, 88, p1041-1054.

Sheehan, M. Oppenheimer, E. and Taylor, C. (1986) 'Why Drug Users Sought Help From One London Drug Clinic', *British Journal of Addiction*, 81, p765-755.

Smart, R. G. (1976) 'Outcome Studies of Therapeutic and Halfway House Treatment For Addicts', *International Journal of Addictions*, 11, p143-159.

Stimson, G. V. and Oppenheimer, E. (1982) *Heroin Addiction: Treatment and Control in Britain*, Tavistock, Cambridge.

Strang, J. (1988) 'Debates and developments in the treatment of opioid dependence' *Current Opinion in Psychiatry*, 1, p353-360.

Thorley, A. (1981) 'Longitudinal Studies of Drug Dependence', *in* Edwards, G. and Busch, C. (eds.) *Drug Problems in Britain: A Review of Ten Years*, Academic Press, London.

Todhunter, C. Pearson, M. Foley, B. (1992) Merseyside Drugs Council Liverpool Project: The Client's Views, The Centre for Community and Educational Policy Studies and the Department of General Practice, University of Liverpool.

Toon, P. Lynch, R. (1994) 'Changes in therapeutic communities in the UK', *in* Strang, J. Gossop, M. (eds) *Heroin Addiction and Drug Policy: the British System*, Oxford University Press, Oxford.

Vaillant, G.E. (1983) *The Natural History of Alcoholism*, Harvard University Press, Cambridge, MA.

Waldorf, D. and Biernacki, P. (1979) 'Natural recovery from heroin addiction: a review of the incidence literature' *Journal of Drug Issues*, Spring.

Wells, B. (1994) 'Narcotics Anonymous (NA) in Britain', *in* Strang, J. and Gossop, M. (eds) *Heroin Addiction and Drug Policy: the British System*, Oxford Univeristy Press, Oxford.

Yates, A. J. (1990) 'The Natural History of Heroin Addiction', *in* Warburton, D. M. (ed.) *Addiction Controversies*, Harwood, London.

Drugs and the media

by Ross Coomber

Introduction

This chapter will briefly review and explore the relationship between the media and drugs. It is not intended to be exhaustive nor does it seek to provide more than an introduction to many of the issues raised.

The relationship is not a simple one. Messages about drugs are often mixed and contradictory and people do not receive messages from the media passively, simply accepting the views of journalists and politicians without reference to their own experience and beliefs. This situation is further complicated when we consider the *role* of the media. Is it there to inform, to reflect the views of the population, or to stimulate serious debate? It has also been argued that the media is manipulated into playing up and exaggerating drug issues to move the focus away from other sensitive topics, such as unemployment and poverty (Goode and Ben-Yehuda 1994; Kohn 1987; Edelman 1988). These issues will be considered below.

What type of images of drugs and drug users does the media portray?

"Horror as drug addicts' fingers fall off" (*Scottish Sunday Mail*, 12.7.92); "Heroin Kills TV Syd's Son" (*The Sun*, 30.1.95); "Fight Drugs: Addiction leads to misery and death" (*Lewisham Star*, 3.7.86).

Each of these headlines are examples of how the national tabloid and local press commonly build up stories related to drugs and/or drug users. The headlines are powerful and succinct, sticking to the commonly perceived dangers of drugs and what happens if you get mixed up with them. Drug stories are considered by the media to be newsworthy, at least in the sense that they are judged to be of such popular interest that they will attract audiences or readers. But it is not just news-papers and magazines which have a consistent interest. Drug-related themes are also the stuff of many films, documentaries, chat shows, commercials (Government health education campaigns), and television soap operas. Overwhelmingly they tend to present a variation on the images evoked by the headlines above.

It is true however that depending on the medium involved (television, magazines, broadsheet newspapers, tabloids), the approach will tend to vary even if the general message does not. So, for example, a recent report on an ex-steroid user who committed suicide by running head first into a wall while resident in a psychiatric ward was headlined on the front page of the national tabloid *Today* as "Steroids Drove Him Mad ... then Mr Muscles killed himself". In the local newspaper, the front page kept up the drug connection with the headline, "Emotional plea by mother of bodybuilder driven mad by steroid abuse" (*South London Press* 10.3.95). By contrast, *The Guardian* devoted only a small column to the story headed "Man Died After Butting Wall" but then uncritically reported that the individual had used steroids and that this had been cited as sufficient cause. In fact it is by no means certain that the 'quality' broadsheet newspapers are necessarily more reliable, for as Bean (1993: 61) has pointed out in relation to reporting around crack cocaine, "The *Observer* had consistently been the source of some of the most dramatic forms of presentation and indeed misinformation, even overtaking some of the tabloids ... crack was described as 'a highly refined and smokable variant of cocaine, said to be so potent that a single dose can lead to addiction' ... 'this drug crack is a killer. And Britain could be its next target'".

Most drug-related stories, like those above, do not try to present the story within a broader context or question its facts but are happy to blame the drug as sole cause. No consideration for example was given in these stories to the bodybuilder's previous psychiatric disposition or, in the case of crack, whether the reports were consistent with what we know about addiction and the effects of cocaine in general. Assumptions therefore are made about drug effects and their harmful potential which are neither substantiated nor questioned. It is as though there is an underlying assumption that we already know as much as we need to know about drugs and their effects and about drug users and the things they are capable of. This is often taken to its logical conclusion by the common use of 'drug user biographies' – "At nine he was in the playground, at 12 he was sniffing glue, at 22 my son Georgie was dead from an overdose" (*Daily Mirror* 17.10.94) – the unquestioned quoting/interviewing of an ex-drug user or someone close to them – "Once they take it they're hooked for life. People who sell these drugs are murderers and they are evil" (*Guardian* 22.1.94 quoting the distressed mother of a dead heroin addict) – or a highlighted reference to what is often unsubstantiated 'fact' – "Highly addictive and easily obtainable, crack is the fastest growing problem on the drug scene. You may think you can handle it but after one high you are hooked, as 22-year-old student Michele discovered" (*Mizz,* May 1994).

Drug stories can be so useful to certain reporting that even when the drug connection is tenuous to the main story it is not unusual for the drug aspect to be given undue and often misleading prominence. For example, the story which ran under the heading "Drugs Kill Def Leppard Rock Idol Steve" (*Today* 1991), actually reported that the musician died from alcohol poisoning not a drug overdose. Similarly, the headline "Teenager Kim Armitage died after a cocktail of drink and drugs..." (*Daily Express* 1995) arguably suggested use of illicit drugs whereas the drugs in question were in fact "aspirin with her mother's painkillers". Similarly Messner *et al* (1993) illustrate how a story about wife battering in two major daily newspapers framed it as a drugs story while largely ignoring the violence aspect.

Some stories carry with them widely held assumptions about 'street drugs' that journalists feel able to cite with impunity despite almost no evidence: "Ecstasy has turned to agony for thousands of E users as dealers spike tablets and capsules with heroin, LSD, *rat poison and crushed glass* (my emphasis)" (*Time Out* 27.10.93). Although firmly believed even by many drug agency workers and users themselves, the existence of rat poison or crushed glass as adulterants in street drugs is almost unheard of.

Statistics provide another potentially misleading source about the drug scene, when "Official statistics are swallowed whole [and] where official/expert (or not so expert) statements are uncritically treated as reality" (Shapiro 1981).

Media education campaigns

There are often many factual inaccuracies and distortions in media reporting of drugs. For example, in portraying heroin use, popular media in particular will revert to stereotypical images of the heroin user as being invariably spotty, skinny, ill and deceitful, living a life of unremitting crime and degradation leading to the mortuary slab. This view of heroin use was adopted wholesale by the Government's 1985/6 and 1987 drug education campaigns which used conventional 'scare' tactics in an attempt to prevent young people trying drugs. These campaigns were a deliberate attempt to utilise the media as a tool for preventing drug use, by communicating the potential horrors of heroin addiction. While not being 'wrong' (in the sense that the images can and do represent the *consequences* of heroin addiction in many instances) they are unhelpful as a way of understanding much about drug use and addiction. One obvious consequence of these media campaigns was that media reporting of drugs in the more sensationalist forms already discussed was given added credibility. Interestingly, there was anecdotal evidence that some young people found the emaciated image of the boy in the poster campaign which accompanied the TV adverts, rather attractive and used the poster to decorate their bedrooms. The actual research conducted to evaluate the impact of the campaigns indicated that those who were anti-heroin in the first place had their feelings confirmed by the campaign, but there was a nothing to indicate that any sort of scare campaign would actually stop somebody experimenting with the drug.

One unintended effect of scare campaigns which give such massive prominence and visibility to drugs such as heroin is that they may actually *increase* experimentation with these drugs. In its 1984 report on *Prevention* (pp35-36), the Government's own advisory body, the Advisory Council on the Misuse of Drugs (ACMD) warned, "Whilst we accept the need, in appropriate circumstances, for education to include factual information about drugs and their effects, we are concerned about measures which deliberately present information in a way which is intended to shock or scare. We believe that educational programmes based on such measures on their own are likely to be ineffective or, at the very worst, positively harmful". Research elsewhere has supported this fear (De Haes 1987; Schaps *et al* 1981). Thus, to some young people, branding the use of mysterious and dangerous substances as anti-social and deviant may (especially if they have seen peers using these drugs with few of the effects sensationalised by the media) provide a focus and new outlet through which their frustrations may be vented and their 'resistance' demonstrated, while for others it may merely spark their curiosity.

The language of drug reporting

When it comes to presenting the drug issue to the public there is a common vocabulary with recurrent metaphors which inform the statements and reports not only of the press, but also national and local politicans, medical experts, and many others. Two of the most consistent metaphors are the drug 'epidemic' – the disease running unchecked across the land contaminating all it touches – and the 'war' against drugs where gung-ho language such as 'fight', 'battle', 'onslaught on the drugs epidemic' (all from one story, *Evening Standard* 22.4.94) is used to reassure the public that the sternest possible law and order response is in place to deal with the problem.

The notion of an 'epidemic' is useful because it evokes an image of contamination which cannot be controlled except by the harshest measures – segregation, incarceration, kill or cure. An epidemic is a public health issue, affecting us all. It is not a problem of individuals, but of communities and society. The metaphor completely removes from the picture the active individual, the circumstances under which initial drug experimentation takes place and the context in which continued use is likely to occur – it de-personalises the problem. Epidemics can also be forecasted to achieve all sorts of worrying proportions, and, as we shall see later in relation to crack, be exaggerated out of all proportion to the actual problem.

By using and repeating particular metaphors it has been argued that 'reality' is framed and organised in particular ways, "For example, framing the issue of drug abuse ... by using the 'drug war' metaphor implies a strong application of law enforcement and even military intervention to the problem" (McLeod *et al* 1992) as has happened in the USA (Trebach 1987). On the other hand, a differing emphasis on addiction as a health problem rather than a social one, may frame the issue differently and consequently lead to a helping response instead of a criminal justice one. There was evidence of both these approaches in the UK during the mid-1980s. Concern over the rise in the number of young heroin addicts (seen as victims who needed help) ran parallel to the more traditional reporting about drug traffickers (seen as 'evil merchants of doom' who needed locking up). Thus the media helped create the climate where substantially new resources were made available for treatment and rehabilitation at the same time as restating the public demand for a 'war against drugs' directed at traffickers.

What is the impact of media reporting on attitudes to drugs and drug users?

The oldest debates about the press have centred around its ability to influence people's thinking and attitudes. This debate remains relevant to the drug issue. If most media portrayals of drugs tend to reproduce existing drug mythologies, fail to contextualise drug issues more broadly and sensationalise much of the experience of drug use in society, then we need to consider how important this is to how drug users are generally understood and dealt with.

However, trying to actually determine the impact of the press on attitudes to particular issues is far from easy. Certainly, the aptly named 'hypodermic syringe model' – which has it that audiences are directly and predictably influenced by the media, information being pumped into the body of the population and absorbed – is inappropriate in this case. On the other hand many surveys about drugs show that most people's main source of information about drugs is the popular media (Coggans 1991).

Most media output is intended to be informative or entertaining. Research which has attempted to find out how much the media can inform and educate, and therefore alter or even reinforce existing beliefs, has shown that media effects are complex. Different status, class, gender and cultural groups receive information differently and do different things with it (Morley 1980; Tichenor *et al* 1970; Cantril 1940). Despite this complexity, there are a number of areas where media influence appears able to have impacts which are relevant to our discussion.

Firstly and most obviously, the general public is unusually dependent on the media for information about any new phenomenon (Katz & Lazarsfeld 1955; Glover 1984). A recent example of this, the emergence of HIV/AIDS in the early 1980s, led to all sorts of negative images and press sensationalism ('gay plague') providing false messages and information that proved difficult to dislodge, even from some health care workers years after more reliable information was known. This also indicates that initial and fearful images may in some cases be relatively resistant to future alternative messages.

Secondly, it's hardly surprising that existing views and attitudes are easily reinforced, particularly because of the cumulative exposure to similar images in newspapers, television, books and films going back decades. What is significant is that alternative messages, although they occasionally surface, are comfortably countered by the weight of messages which reinforce existing perceptions. This is particularly true when combined with a topic or subject upon which individuals are almost entirely reliant on the media for their information. Finally, the language and metaphors used by the media may help frame the way a problem is seen and help set the agenda for how it should be dealt with.

Moral panics

One further recurrent theme around drugs and the media is that of the 'moral panic' or the media-led drug scare. In this scenario, the media are able to create a scare through the reporting of drug-related concerns disproportionate to the actual seriousness of the problem. Scares may originate from an increase in Customs and Excise drug seizures or the arrival of a 'new' drug.

The theory of the moral panic was originally developed by Stan Cohen (1972) in relation to the fears around violence between 'Mods' and 'Rockers' in the 1960s. Cohen sought to explain how a relatively small and isolated social problem (a clash of the two groups in a seaside town over a Bank Holiday weekend) was exaggerated in the media to something more. The stories were spiced up with the dark imagery of leather jackets and motorbike gangs suggesting that the seriousness of the incident was actually related to the type of individual involved and the fear that such behaviour and 'fashions' among the young would become a broad threat to society as a whole.

The consequences of a moral panic are that it creates an 'amplification spiral' with the police, courts, government and the general public becoming less tolerant of the behaviour depicted. Similar styles, fashions and images often get sucked into the vortex and an isolated incident becomes more broadly defined. This results in the creation of new social controls (laws, restrictions) constructed as a response to the problem as conceived. Explicit in most theories of moral panic is the idea that the focus of the panic (the group involved) serves to identify 'folk-devils' (e.g. junkies) who are then scapegoated as examples of what is wrong with society and provides a target onto which general fears and anxieties may be pinned.

The crack cocaine scare of the late 1980s occurred during an ongoing anti-drugs campaign (predominately heroin) and resulted in what Bean (1993: 59) describes as a drug scare without parallel in all those that have "beset the British drug scene over the last 25 years". This was despite the fact that little evidence of any significant increase in use was available in Britain. The scare elicited overstatement from all quarters – neither the quality press, television news nor tabloids were immune. Bean (1993) similarly suggests that the crack scare in Britain was media-*led*, based on speculative assumptions about instant addiction, a ready and existing demand, and the notion that problems which emerge in the USA have a strong likelihood of surfacing here. The epidemic never happened and the National Task Force set up to outmanoeuvre and deal with the expected problem was disbanded two and half years later through relative inactivity. It was however indicative of what the media could do with a drug issue. US drug enforcement agents forecasted a crack explosion in Britain and hyped the drug as having previously unseen powers. The media chose not to question the reliability of these predictions but to accept them unconditionally. The situation in Britain in 1995 is that crack does have a significant presence in areas of traditional drug use, such as deprived inner-city areas, and does cause many problems. However, the dire predictions about the end of British society as we know it have thankfully not been proved correct.

The impact of panics on public attitudes is borne out by research. Reeves and Campbell (1994) relate how in the USA in the mid-1980s the media-led crack scare helped produce a jump in public opinion on drugs as the nation's most important problem from two per cent to 13 per cent over the five month period of mass coverage. Beckett (1994) has described how public fears and anxieties over crime and drugs are often transformed by panics led and constructed by the media, and others have described similar media-inspired drug scares elsewhere, especially in America (Goode & Ben-Yehuda, 1994; Trebach, 1987; Reinerman & Levine, 1989).

Why does the media present such images?

So far we have looked at the type of drug-related image presented in the media and considered how useful they are as a means of understanding drug use. We then considered the effects of these representations and found that although 'effects' as such are difficult to measure there are circumstances where they are more likely to occur, such as when new information becomes available. We also have to recognise that in general, the media (or at least the *news* media) is aware that it can influence attitudes and behaviour and accordingly tries to reflect that responsibility in the manner of its information provision. We then have to ask *why* does the news media report drugs in the way that it does? At the very least there appear to be three interrelated factors which may partly explain how and why such reporting has come to pass: the construction of 'the dope fiend', the importance of the 'human-interest' story, and the view that the media acts as a 'mirror' to society.

The dope fiend

For much of the 19th century there was little concern over the very common use of opium and it was taken widely as a form of self-medication for a wide range of ailments. From the 1830s a number of factors came together which fundamentally altered public perceptions of opium and the type of person who used it. Fears were soon raised around the displacement of alcohol by opium amongst the working classes and its use for 'stimulation' rather than for medication. Such use was considered as a societal threat despite little or no evidence to support this belief (Berridge and Edwards 1987).

These fears later coincided with and were bolstered by the claims of the emerging medical and pharmaceutical professions that opium was too dangerous a drug to be available for self-medication and that there should be controls (medical and pharmaceutical, of course) over its use. This came about because of genuine concerns over the rise in the number of infant poisonings, but opium and other drugs also became the battleground over which doctors and pharmacists fought for control of the prescription of drugs.

There was also a much more unpleasant concern – that of a perceived threat to society from outside. From the 1860s, interest grew in the numerically small but highly concentrated and visible Chinese immigrant population in London. And as far as the media of the time was concerned, wherever there was a Chinaman, there was an opium den. Literature was riddled with the drug and its effects, from Dicken's *Mystery of Edwin Drood* (1870) to Oscar Wilde's *Picture of Dorian Gray* (1891) and Conan Doyle's Sherlock Holmes stories. Opium smoking was depicted in these books "in a manner soon accepted as reality ... 'fantastic postures on ragged mattresses. The twisted limbs, the gaping mouths, the staring lustreless eyes' ... Not all writers were so obviously hostile; yet from the 1870s an increasing tone of racial and cultural hostility was discernable" (Berridge and Edwards 1987:197). Opium was blamed for the failure of missionaries to convert the Chinese to Christianity, and the use of opium for pleasure became linked to depravity and weakness. The ever-present Victorian fear of 'racial contamination' was only heightened by the newly-perceived fear of opium.

Similar issues had also emerged in America in the 1870s, where there was a much larger Chinese population. Kohn (1992: 2) notes that "Variations on this scene set the tone of the British drug panic of the 1920s, firing on the potent juxtaposition of young white women, 'men of colour' (the term was current), sex and drugs. If the ultimate menace of drugs had to be summarised in a single proposition, it would be that they facilitated the seduction of young white women by men of other races". Between 1910 and 1930 Parssinen (1983: 115) reports "In newspapers, fiction and films, the public was deluged with a mass of fact and opinion about drugs. The perception of danger expressed in ...the previous four decades, gave way to near hysteria". In America other racist images of blacks, Mexicans and Chinese were being spread by zealots such as Hamilton Wright who propagated stories about black cocaine users who once intoxicated, raped white women and could only be halted by a hail of bullets (Musto 1987). In England, headlines demonstrated similar fears: "White Girls 'Hypnotised' by Yellow Men", "The Lure of the Yellow

Man – English Girls' Moral Suicide – Fatal Fascination" (Kohn 1992: 3). With the First World War furnishing reporters with the opportunity to combine drug scare stories with those of alien conspiracies and spies (Kohn 1992) the construction of the drug fiend and the powers of 'dope' were as firmly entrenched as the troops in France.

By the 1930s in America, it was the turn of other drugs to be 'demonised'. Harry Anslinger, head of the newly-formed Narcotics Bureau, saw drug use as deplorable and degenerate but, more importantly, needed a 'good drug scare' to keep funds coming in from the US Congress (Himmelstein 1983). Anslinger's descriptions of the effects of cannabis seem astounding to us now, but as Gossop (1993) observes they also satisfied a need: "The smallest dose he told his eager audience, was likely to cause fits of raving madness, sexual debauchery, violence and crime". 'Scientific' evidence such as this presented by a highly placed US official, did much to exacerbate how drugs (even comparatively benign ones like cannabis) came to be viewed by the media. The descriptions of addicts at times read like science fiction, but these descriptions came from law courts (Wisotsky 1991), public officials and doctors, not scriptwriters. In the decades that followed, the connection between drugs and 'others' (foreigners) or 'outsiders' (deviants) was continuously reinforced (Bean 1974) and often acted as a catalyst for action against drug users.

The dope fiend had been born, and once such reporting was underway (and it would have been deemed proper and responsible to inform the public of such evils), the familiar media stereotypes became set in stone. They then became increasingly the common currency of drug reporting, reliant on the framework employed in the reporting of human interest stories and the problems attendant in that reporting.

Human interest stories

Curran *et al* (1980: 306) have argued that human interest stories, are a type which show that life is "strongly governed by luck, fate, and chance [and] shares common universal experiences: birth, love, death, accident, illness, and, crucially, the experience of consuming". They seek to reach the maximum audiences through appealing to the lowest common denominator; they "cross the barriers of sex, class, and age, appealing almost equally to all types of reader" (p301). This, they argue, is true of the so-called quality papers as well as the tabloids. A similar approach can be seen in even highly regarded news programmes, such as the News at Ten, which recently introduced an 'And finally.....' section into its broadcasting. This explicitly attempts to end a normal broadcast of doom and gloom (unemployment, civil wars, famines etc) with a happy, lighthearted human interest story. Typical human interest stories are looking to 'hook' the audience, with a certain amount of 'professional licence' applied to the material and its presentation. Curran *et al* argues that commercial pressure since the early 1920s has led to a particular style of news reporting that needs to attract attention and appeal. Drugs stories are only one of many topics (along with sex, crime, scandal and dead donkeys) which are considered to do both. Drugs issues fit neatly into the human interest story formula, even (as we have seen) turning stories which may have little saleable 'interest' into drug stories in an effort to spice them up and increase audiences.

Whose media is it anyway?

The six-million dollar question has to be 'who controls the media' – whose views does it reflect? Sometimes the answer is easy. In the Soviet Union the media was state-run and most of its presentations paid homage to the ideas and propaganda of the Communist Party (Lane 1990). But in democratic societies like Britain and America the debate continues over whether media output is independent, supportive of 'capitalist' ideas, influenced and manipulated by government or by media tycoons. The debate is too lengthy and contorted to rehearse here but one aspect, the idea of the media as mirror, is important.

In relation to a subject like drugs, this would suggest that for the most part the media provides us with images and perspectives which are in line with reasoned public and authoritative thinking, and is therefore responsibly acting in the public interest. And indeed, much of what the media is itself fed, in the form of press releases, public comment, and Government campaigns, contain images which are not inconsistent with what the media then passes on to us. In this sense the media may be said to be providing legitimate and responsible images, and rather than trying to agitate and challenge what is a general consensus on drugs, merely reflects what people already believe. If this is true (and it undoubtedly is in part) then – when combined with the reporting style of the human interest story and the dope fiend stereotype – we can begin to understand why so many drug stories take the form they do and why they continue to do so.

Conclusions

Obviously there are many dangers and problems associated with drug use but the media consistently represents them in ways which distort and fail to adequately contextualise them. This in turn often results in misleading and uninformative images and text.

Why should this matter? Shouldn't people have the worst possible image of drugs? Putting aside the ethical issue of misleading the public, one of the main problems with scare tactics is the impact they have on drug users and the way they may be treated by family, police, the courts and employers. It may for example, prevent them and their families seeking help because of the stigma attached to drug use.

If the role of the media is in any sense to live up to the ideal where "access to relevant information affecting the public good is widely available, where discussion is free ... [and where] the media facilitates this process by providing an arena of public debate" (Curran 1991), then in regard to drugs, there is plenty of room for improvement.

Bibliography

Advisory Council on the Misuse of Drugs (ACMD) (1984) *Prevention*, HMSO, London.

Bean, P. (1974) *The social control of drugs*, Martin Robertson, London.

Bean, P. (1993) 'Cocaine and Crack: The Promotion of an Epidemic', *in* Bean, P. (ed.) *Cocaine and Crack: Supply and Use*, Macmillan.

Beckett, K. (1994) 'Setting the Public Agenda: "Street Crime" and Drug Use in American Politics', *Social Problems*, 41, 3, pp425-447.

Berridge, V. and Edwards, G. (1987) *Opium and the People*, Yale University Press, London.

Cantril, H. (1940) *The Invasion From Mars: A Study in the Psychology of Panic*, Princeton University Press, Princeton.

Cohen, S. (1972) *Folk Devils and Moral Panics: The Creation of the Mods and Rockers*, MacGibbon & Kee, London.

Coggans, N *et al* (1991) *National evaluation of drug education in Scotland*. London: ISDD.

Curran, J. Douglas, A. and Whannel, G. (1980) 'The Political Economy of the Human-Interest Story', *in* Smith, A. (*ed.*) *Newspapers and Democracy: International Essays on a Changing Medium*, Massachusetts Institute of Technology Press, Cambridge, Massachusetts.

Curran, J. *et al* (1991) 'Mass media and democracy: a reappraisal' *in* Curran, J. and Gurevitch, M. *Mass media and society*, Edward Arnold, London.

De Haes, W. (1987) 'Looking for Effective Drug Education Programmes: Fifteen Years Exploration of the Effects of Different Drug Education Programmes', *Health Education Research*, 2. 4, pp433-438.

Edelman, M. (1988) *Constructing The Political Spectacle,* University of Chicago Press, Chicago.

Glover, D. (1984) *The Sociology of the Mass Media*, Causeway Books, Lancs.

Goode, E. and Ben-Yehuda, N. (1994) *Moral Panics: The Construction of Deviance*, Blackwell, Cambridge Massachusetts.

Gossop, M. (1993) *Living With Drugs*, 3rd Edition, Ashgate, Aldershot.

Himmelstein, J.L. (1983) *The strange career of marihuana*. Greenwood Press. Westport, Conn.

Katz, E. and Lazarsfeld, P. (1955) *Personal Influence*, The Free Press, New York.

Kohn, M. (1987) *Narcomania: On Heroin,* Faber and Faber, London.

Kohn, M. (1992) *Dope Girls: The Birth of the British Underground*, Lawrence & Wishart, London.

Lane, D. (1990) *Soviet Society Under Perestroika*, Unwin Hyman, London.

McLeod, J. M., Kosicki, G. M. and Pan, Z. (1992) 'On Understanding and Misunderstanding Media Effects', *in* Curran, J. and Gurevitch, M. *Mass Media and Society*, Edward Arnold, Guildford.

Messner, M. A. (1993) 'Outside the Frame: Newspaper Coverage of the Sugar Ray Leonard Wife Abuse Story', *Sociology of Sport*, 10, 2, June, pp119-134.

Morley, D. (1980) *The 'Nationwide' Audience,* British Film Institute, London.

Musto, D. (1987) *The American Disease: Origins of Narcotic Control*, 2nd edition, Oxford University Press, Oxford.

Parssinen, T. M. (1983) *Secret Passions, Secret Remedies: Narcotic Drugs in British Society 1820-1930*, Manchester University Press, Manchester.

Reinerman, C. and Levine, H. G. (1989) 'The Crack Attack: Politics and Media in America's Latest Drug Scare', *in* Best, J. (ed.) *Images of Issues*, Aldine Press.

Reeves, J. L. and Campbell, R. (1994) *Cracked Coverage: Television News, The Anti-Cocaine Crusade, and the Reagan Legacy*, Duke University Press, Durham.

Schaps, E. DiBartolo, R. Moskowitz, J. Palley, C. S. and Churgin, S. (1981) 'A Review of 127 Drug Abuse Prevention Programme Evaluations', *Journal of Drug Issues*, pp17-43.

Shapiro, H. (1981) 'Press Review July 1980 – May 1981', *Druglink*, Summer 1981, ISDD.

Trebach, A. S. (1987) *The Great Drug War: And Radical Proposals Which Could Make America Safe Again*, Macmillan, New York.

Tichenor, P. J. Donohue, G. A. and Olien, C. N. (1970) 'Mass Media Flow and Differential Growth in Knowledge', *Public Opinion Quarterly*, 34, pp159-170.

Wisotsky, S. (1991) 'Not thinking like a lawyer': the case of drugs in the courts. *In* Notre Dame Journal of Law, *Ethic and Public Policy*: 5 (3).

Drug Myths

by Ross Coomber

Introduction

A myth is a popular belief which has limited use as a way of understanding the subject on which it is focused. While there are often elements of truth in all myths, in the main it could be said that they are based on stereotypical and simplistic images which have their roots in ignorance, and attribute particular characteristics to things and people which are neither supported nor substantiated by much more than hearsay. Furthermore, there are more often than not consequences (some good, some bad) for those they focus on.

Drug myths fit this description quite well. If drug users are classified as degenerate rather than in need of help they will be treated in ways appropriate to degenerates. They may be subject to harsh criminal laws instead of liberal ones; they may be feared and castigated by their friends, neighbours and community instead of accepted or supported; they may be scapegoated because of what they do and who they are. In short, by 'demonising' the drugs, invariably the same happens to those people who use them.

There are many myths about drugs. Some like 'once an addict always an addict' have been covered elsewhere in this *Reader*. Below, we outline a few of the hardier myths about the misuse of drugs.

Hard versus soft drugs

The terms 'hard' and 'soft' suggest the inherent dangers of using a particular drug. A 'hard' drug is associated with a variety of potential dangers ranging from helpless addiction to mindless violence. Heroin and cocaine are considered to be hard drugs.

Drugs such as cannabis, ecstasy, and amphetamines are generally considered to be 'soft' drugs because the effects are considered to be comparatively less intoxicating, less likely to lead to addiction and less likely to be dangerous for the user in general. Sounds simple enough, doesn't it? And that's the problem – not only is it too simple a way of categorising drugs, but in the light of some basic information about the drug scene as a whole, it does not stand up to much scrutiny.

Extrapolating the 'hard/soft' argument, legal drugs such as alcohol and tobacco and drugs such as paracetamol which are available in any corner shop, must be softer than the 'softest' illicit drug, otherwise they wouldn't be so widely available. Yet the dangers of misusing these drugs are well documented. Paracetamol is an effective painkiller, but in 1991 over 200 people died from paracetamol overdose. The prescribing of over-the-counter tranquillisers often results in unwanted side effects and may lead to some form of dependence in over a third of prescribing cases (Gabe and Williams 1986). Research has suggested that significant numbers of hospital prescriptions result in a "*major* toxic reaction" to the medicine prescribed (Gossop 1993: 49).

Tobacco alone is believed to be responsible for 110,000 premature deaths in Britain annually (HEA 1991), as well as significantly contributing to thousands of cases of heart disease, thrombosis and cancer. Alcohol is considered to cause between five and 25,000 premature deaths a year and like tobacco is associated with serious health problems for many thousands more. Using the rationale of hard/soft drugs outlined at the beginning, these drugs would have to be designated as 'hard' yet the hard/soft distinction is never applied to them in the general debate about drugs.

Risk of death is one of the benchmarks by which we label a drug as dangerous, but the number of deaths attributed to *illicit* drugs is far less than commonly thought. Even allowing for the fact that there are far fewer users of heroin than alcohol or tobacco, a smaller proportion of heroin users are likely to die from their drug of choice than smokers and drinkers. Granted, there is a far greater risk of overdosing on heroin than alcohol and dependence is likely to take hold far more quickly than alcohol or tobacco. However, in terms of toxicity, heroin, unlike alcohol or tobacco, does not damage major organs of the body such as the heart, liver or brain and tolerance to huge doses can be built up where even decades of use result in no discernable physical damage from the drug itself. (A regular and reliable supply of heroin may be taken with relatively little impact on the user. It is when supply is interrupted that problems are likely to be encountered.) The main dangers (dependence or overdose apart) relate to *how* the drug is taken. Thus the use of dirty or contaminated needles present dangers as great as the drug itself.

The historical and cultural context in which drug use takes place also influences the hard/soft distinction. There was a time in the 1960s and '70s in America, for example, when cocaine was viewed as a relatively benign drug which caused few problems. The advent of crack radically changed this perspective.

By contrast cannabis in the 1950s was associated with numerous harmful attributes, including powerful addictive properties, violence-inducing tendencies and the likelihood of producing both moral and physical degeneration. Today, these views have very little credibility. Undoubtedly cannabis would have been considered a 'hard' drug in the 1950s whereas in the 1990s it is generally seen as a 'soft' one.

Another problem with the oppositional separation into 'hard' and 'soft', is that it may conjure up an image of soft drugs as harmless. All drugs have some level of danger attached to their use. Ecstasy use has been associated with a number of deaths in recent years (Newcombe 1994) mainly related to heatstroke when combined with long periods of intense dancing. Amphetamine use can lead to a range of problems (tiredness, delusions, paranoia, psychosis, addiction) depending on the regularity and severity of use. Amphetamine is considered a soft drug yet its effects are similar to those of cocaine. Cannabis smoke appears to be more damaging than cigarette smoke in relation to respiratory complaints and diseases, while an inexperienced LSD user may suffer distressing psychological effects from the 'trip'. Solvents, barely considered in the ambit of 'soft drugs', in reality kill substantially more young people in the 12-19 age group than all the other substances put together (Taylor *et al* 1994; HOSB 1993).

Finally, the categorisation of drugs into soft and hard is often a reflection of what is also a politically expedient approach to understanding drugs. Historically, groups lobbying for the legalisation or the decriminalisation of cannabis have sought to distinguish the drug from 'harder' ones by claiming cannabis to be a drug with few attendant problems compared to the severity of harm caused by drugs like heroin. Similarly, the anti-drug lobby constructs an image of illicit drugs whereby soft drugs are shown to be no better than hard drugs because they seduce the user to seek the stronger, more intense experiences promised by their more dangerous relatives.

Using soft drugs leads to hard drugs

Another reason why certain illicit drugs are sometimes referred to as soft and hard relates to the long-held belief that experimentation with or regular use of certain drugs (particularly cannabis) will lead – as sure as night follows day – to the use of 'harder' drugs. The theory goes that the user is exposed to drugtaking, is seduced by its pleasures and moves on to bigger and better things. It is in this way that drugs such as cannabis and amphetamines are seen as being 'gateway' or 'stepping-stone' drugs. However, the relationship and transition between different drugs is not quite as simple as this.

While studies consistently show that nearly all heroin addicts have used cannabis it is also clear that only a small minority of cannabis users will 'progress' to hard drug use. If this were not true, then there would be many more heroin users given the millions who have ever tried cannabis (perhaps eight million people in Britain alone). A recent Government survey found that although 96 per cent of people who had used opiates in the past year had also taken cannabis, only seven per cent of cannabis users had taken opiates (Leitner *et al* 1993: 203). There is as much of a causal link between cannabis use and heroin use as there is between a young person drinking shandy and a tramp drinking meths – they may be at opposite ends of a spectrum but that doesn't mean there is a clear progression from one to the other.

Although it is true that cannabis use is the most common first *illegal* drug to be used, most cannabis users have already 'experimented' with tobacco and alcohol, both of which have significant psychoactive and physiological effects. In fact many heavy cannabis users never try drugs such as heroin, and often exhibit the same negative prejudices and accept some of the stereotypes about heroin users as other members of the non drug-using population.

Gossop (1993: 103) makes the ironic point that maybe the number of cannabis users who experiment with other drugs is swollen by the simple fact that in order to get hold of cannabis, users have to mix with dealers who may supply other drugs and are tempted to experiment with them much more than if the current controls on cannabis did not make this association necessary.

That said, there clearly are cannabis users who do move on to heroin. There are also social drinkers who go on to become alcoholics. The point however is that there is nothing inevitable about this 'progression'.There is nothing inherent in cannabis or a glass of wine which propels people up (or down) an inevitable slope.

The pusher at the school gate

"Playground pushers are selling amphetamines disguised as jelly beans to schoolkids" (*The People* 17.10.93).

One of the most common and hardy drug myths is that of the evil pusher at the school gates or some other opportunist place (the ice cream van is another favourite) enticing vulnerable young children into drug use in order to increase their sales. There is little, if indeed any, evidence to support such a view. In reality, there are a number of amalgamated myths which help construct this particular picture. One such long-standing myth is the idea that the dealer will provide free samples in order to 'hook' the child, and that once hooked the child will bring a new and regular income. There are a couple of problems with this scenario:

1. Most schoolchildren do not have a regular and sufficient income to actually become dependent on drugs which can be a lengthy and expensive process.

2. Pushing drugs onto schoolchildren would also present an unreasonable risk to

the seller. Parents and teachers would soon learn of such a character and act accordingly.

Although there is little research on drug dealing in schools, it is likely that where drugs are available in school, it will be one of the students who has access to them and is either dealing to make a bit of cash or selling their own excess to friends.

There has always been a fear of the unscrupulous and degenerate character preying on the weakest for their own gain. The fact that the archetypal 'pusher' is not found or caught rarely disproves to believers that he did not exist in the first place. Unfortunately for the mythmakers, initial and early drug use has little to do with pushers as they are conventionally portrayed. Initial provision of an illicit drug is nearly always from within the peer group (friends and acquaintances) or the family (an older brother or sister). It is unlikely that unknown 'pushers' would have much success enticing people into drug use as they are not equipped with the 'security' of the peer/kin group, which gives the drug credibility and desirability, and provide a setting in which it can be taken and learned about, thereby providing a context in which second, third and continuing use can occur.

This persistent mythology sets up parents and children to resist temptation from evil strangers, but this can divert attention from the settings where experimentation is most likely to occur. Friends, friends of friends, relatives and neighbours are not drug fiends, but they are more likely to be the source of drug experimentation than a menacing figure in shadow and shades.

Instant or inevitable addiction

The notion that certain drugs have the power to make individuals immediately crave them and compel them towards more use and inevitable addiction is yet another drug fallacy. Recently we have heard much about the powers of crack cocaine to produce instant addiction. This is not the first time a drug has been given such a press. Heroin is another drug to which such powers are often attributed: an American book was titled *It's So Good Don't Even Try it Once*.

In reality, the process of becoming dependent on heroin, for example, is quite lengthy and relies on a number of factors related to personal circumstances. Most people who try it for the first time are physically sick and won't bother again. Others will try it a few times and then decide heroin isn't for them. If you carry on taking the drug, tolerance builds up so that you need higher and more frequent doses to get the same effect. If you got to the point where you were using the drug on a daily basis and then suddenly stopped using it, you would experience the classic heroin withdrawal symptoms. This would mean your body has become physically dependent on heroin and you feel ill if you stop using. To feel 'normal' you would need to take more heroin. Even then for somebody to reach the point where they are so hooked on heroin both physically and psychologically that it completely dominates their life can take several months (Kaplan 1983).

The effects of smoking crack cocaine are very different to smoking or injecting heroin, but many of the lessons are the same. Dependence on any drug does not occur solely because of the drug's effects. Although crack cocaine provides a quick and intense euphoria and dependence *may* occur more quickly than to cocaine powder, to become addicted to crack (a psychological addiction in this case) an individual has to be 'dedicated' to the daily ritual of obtaining money for drugs, arranging to buy them, use them, come down from the effects and start all over again. 'Crack' is one of the more recent drugs to be labelled 'instantly addictive', but there is enough research evidence to show that many people do not enjoy the crack experience and fail to repeat it, while others can 'take it or leave it', primarily because to acquire a 'crack habit' means finding hundreds of pounds every week (Ditton and Hammersley 1994; Miller 1991; Newcombe 1989). The association with instant addiction and this particular drug may say more about the type of user *most visible* in the American experience. Research into freebase cocaine users and some crack users suggests that many are in fact more heavily involved in heavy and multiple drug use than other users. Thus the scare over the powers of crack may have been exacerbated by the *visibility* of existing heavy drug users using a new drug (crack) to excess and apparently demonstrating its ability to hook quickly and easily those people already heavily involved in a drug-using lifestyle.

The pain of withdrawal

A common myth about heroin dependence is that the pain of withdrawal is unbearable and even life-threatening. This is probably a major reason why many heroin users are scared of giving up the drug and it also helps reinforce the notion that heroin is a drug which enslaves users for ever, or at least until they die. Abrupt withdrawal from some drugs such as alcohol, barbiturates and tranquillisers can be highly dangerous, but for many users the effects of withdrawing from heroin are similar to a very bad dose of flu – not very pleasant, but hardly life-threatening.

Of course physically withdrawing from the drug so that it is no longer in the body, is only the beginning of the process of coming off drugs. As one musician said many years ago about heroin, "they can get it out of your body, but they can't get it out of your mind". Although this is an exaggeration, it is true that rehabilitation is a long process involving major changes of attitude, motivation, lifestyle and so on, so that drugs are no longer the central feature of a person's life.

Bibliography

Ditton, J. and Hammersley, R. (1994) 'The typical cocaine user', *Druglink*, November/December, ISDD.

Dorn, N. Murji, K. and South, N. (1992) *Traffickers: Drug Markets and Law Enforcement*, Routledge, London.

Gabe, J. and Williams, P. (eds.) (1986) *Tranquillisers: Social, Psychological and Clinical Perspectives*, Tavistock, London.

Ghodse, A. H. 'Morbidity and mortality', *in* Edwards, G. and Busch, C. (eds.) (1981) *Drug Problems in Britain*, Academic Press, London.

Ghodse, A. H. Sheenan, M. Taylor, C. Edwards, G. (1985) 'Deaths of drug addicts in the united Kingdom 1967-1981', *British Medical Journal*, 290: 425-428.

Gossop, M. (1993) *Living with Drugs* (3rd edition), Arena, Cambridge.

Health Education Authority (1991) *The smoking epidemic: counting the cost in England*, HEA, London.

Home Office Statistical Bulletin (1993) *Statistics of drug addicts notified to the Home Office, United Kingdom 1992*. Issue 15/93, 27 May.

Kaplan, J. (1983) *The Hardest drug: Heroin and Public Policy*, University of Chicago Press, Chicago.

Leitner M. *et al.* (1993) *Drug usage and drugs prevention: the views and habits of the general public*, HMSO, London.

Miller, R. M. (1991) *The Case for Legalising Drugs*, Praeger, Westport.

Newcombe, R. and Matthews, L. (1989) 'Crack in Liverpool', *Druglink*, September/October, p16.

Newcombe, R. (1994) *Ecstasy Deaths and Other Fatalities Related to Dance Drugs and Raving*, Information Document 4, 3D Research Bureau, Liverpool.

Taylor, J.C. Norman, C.L. Bland, J.M. Anderson, H.R. and Ramsey, J.D. (1994) *Trends in deaths associated with abuse of volatile substances 1971-1992*, Report No 7, St George's Hospital Medical School, London.

Tyler, A. (1986) *Street Drugs: The facts explained. The myths exploded*, (Revised edition), New English Library, Suffolk.

Viscusi, W. K. (1993) *Smoking: Making the Risky Decision*, Oxford University Press, Oxford.

Yates, A.J. (1990) 'The Natural History of Heroin Addiction' *in* Warburton, D.M. (*ed*) *Addiction Controversies*, London.

Reading list

You may want to find out more about the issues covered in this book. The articles and publications listed below represent only a fraction of what is available in ISDD's world-class library.

Chapter 1: Illicit drugs and their effects

Coomber R. (1994) *Drugs and drug use in society – a critical reader.* London: Greenwich University Press.

Drug abuse briefing. 5th edition. (1994) London: ISDD.

Glass I. (*ed*) (1991) *The international handbook of addiction behaviour.* London: Tavistock/ Routledge.

Gossop M. (1987) *Living with drugs. 2nd edition.* Aldershot: Wildwood House.

Hanson G., Venturelli P. (1995) *Drugs and society. 4th edition.* Boston: Jones & Bartlett.

Inaba D., Cohen W. (1993) *Uppers, downers, all arounders: physical and mental effects of psychoactive drugs. 2nd edition.* Oregon: CNS Productions.

Jacobs M.R. *et al* (1987) *Drugs and drug abuse – a reference text. 2nd edition.* Toronto: Addiction Research Foundation.

Lowinson J. *et al* (1992) *Substance abuse: a comprehensive textbook.* London: Williams & Wilkins.

Saunders N. (1993) *E for ecstasy.* London: published by author.

Shulgin A., Shulgin A. (1991) *Pihkal – a chemical love story.* Berkeley, California: Transform Press.

Snyder S.H. (1986) *Drugs and the brain.* New York: Scientific American Library.

Tyler A. (1995) *Street drugs. 3rd edition.* London: Hodder & Stoughton.

Weil A., Rosen W. (1993) *From chocolate to morphine. 2nd edition.* Boston: Houghton Mifflin.

Chapter 2: Why people use drugs

Barnard M., McKeganey N. (1994) *Drug misuse and young people: a selective review of the literature.* Glasgow: Centre for Drug Misuse Research.

Coggans N., McKellar S. (1994) "Drug use amongst peers: peer pressure or peer preference?" *Drugs Education, Prevention and Policy*: 1(1), p15-26.

Davies J. B. (1992) *The myth of addiction: an application of the psychological theory of attribution to illicit drug use.* Reading: Harwood.

Denton R.E, Kampfe C. M. (1994) "The relationship between family variables and adolescent substance abuse: a literature review." *Adolescence*: 29 (114), p475-495.

Edwards G., Lader M. (*eds*) (1990) *The nature of drug dependence.* Oxford: Oxford University Press.

Giggs J. (1991) "Epidemiology of contemporary drug abuse" *in* Whynes D., Bean P. (*eds*) *Policing and prescribing: the British system of drug control.* London: Macmillan. p145-175.

Lettieri D. J., Sayers M., Pearson H. (1980) *Theories on drug abuse: selected contemporary perspectives.* Rockville, Md: National Institute on Drug Abuse.

Chapter 3: How many drug users are there?

Baker O., Marsden J. (1995) *Drug misuse in Britain 1994.* London: ISDD.

Leitner M. *et al* (1993) *Drug usage and drugs prevention: the views and habits of the general public.* London: Home Office Drugs Prevention Initiative.

Mott J., Mirrlees-Black C. (1993) *Self-reported drug misuse in England and Wales: main findings from the 1992 British Crime Survey.* London: Home Office Research and Statistics Department.

Parker H. *et al* (1995) *Drugs futures.* London: ISDD.

Chapter 4: How do drugs affect the family?

Cohen J., Kay J. (1994) *Taking drugs seriously: a parents' guide to young people's drug use.* London: Thorsons.

Dorn N. *et al* (1994) *Coping with a nightmare – family feelings about long-term drug use. 2nd edition.* London: ISDD.

Dorn N. *et al* (1988) "The rise and fall of family support groups". *Druglink* 3(1), p8-11.

Kaufman E., Kaufman P. (1992) *Family therapy of drug and alcohol abuse. 2nd edition.* London: Allyn and Bacon.

Swadi H.S. (1988) "Adolescent drug taking: role of family and peers". *Drug and Alcohol Dependence* 21(2), p157-160.

Velleman R. *et al* (1993) "The families of problem drug users: a study of 50 close relatives". *Addiction* 88(9), p1281-1289.

Chapter 5: Drugs and crime

Bennett T.H., Wright R. (1986) 'The impact of prescribing on the crimes of opioid users', *British Journal of Addiction* 81: 265-73.

Inciardi J.A. (1981) *The Drugs/Crime Connection*, Beverly Hills, CA: Sage.

Johnson B.D. *et al* (1985) *Taking care of business: the economics of crime by heroin abusers.* Lexington: Lexington Books.

Mott J. (1991) "Crime and heroin use" *in* Whynes D., Bean P. *eds. Policing and prescribing: the British system of drug control.* London: Macmillan. p77-94.

Chapter 6: The arguments for and against legalising prohibited drugs

Evans R., Berent I. (1992) *Drug legalization: for and against*. La Salle, Ill: Open Court.

Kleinman M. (1992) *Against excess: drug policy for results*. Basic Books.

Murji K. (1995) "The drug legalisation debate", *Sociology Review*, 4(3), p14-17.

Release (1992) *Release white paper on reform of drug laws*. London: Release.

Chapter 7: Existing drugs strategy across the UK

ACMD *Aids and drug misuse: update* (1993) London: HMSO.

Dorn N. *et al* (1992) *Traffickers – drug markets and law enforcement*. London: Routledge.

Dorn N., South N. (1987) *A land fit for heroin? Drug policies, prevention and practice*. London: Macmillan.

Drugs in Scotland: meeting the challenge (1994) Edinburgh: Scottish Office.

Howard R. *et al* (1993) *Across the divide – building community partnerships to tackle drug misuse*. London: Department of Health.

Strang J., Gossop M. (1994) *Heroin addiction and drug policy – the British system*. Oxford: Oxford University Press.

Tackling drugs together – a strategy for England 1995-1998 (1995) London: HMSO.

Chapter 8: What help is available for drug users and does it work?

ACMD (1982) *Treatment and Rehabilitation: Report of the Advisory Council on the Misuse of Drugs*. London: HMSO.

Farrell M., Ward J., Mattick R. *et al.* (1994) "Methadone maintenance treatment in opiate dependence: a review", *British Medical Journal*, 309, p997-1001.

Fazey C. J. S. (1989) *What works? an evaluation of drug treatments for illicit drug users in the United Kingdom and Europe*. Paper presented at the N.D.R.I. What Works? Conference, New York, USA.

Ghodse H. (1995) *Drugs and addictive behaviour – a guide to treatment. 2nd edition*. Oxford: Blackwell.

Gossop M., Green L., Phillips G. T., Bradley B. (1987) "What happens to opiate addicts immediately after treatment: a prospective follow-up study", *British Medical Journal*, 294, p1377-1380.

Hartnoll R., Power R. (1989) "Why most of Britain's drug users are not looking for help", *Druglink*, March/April, p8-9.

Jarvis T. *et al* (1994) *Treatment approaches for alcohol and drug dependence: an introductory guide*. Chichester: Wiley.

Oppenheimer E., Sheehan M., Taylor, C. (1990) "What happens to drug misusers? A medium-term follow-up of subjects new to treatment", *British Journal of Addiction*, 85, p1255-1260.

Stimson G. V., Oppenheimer E. (1982) *Heroin addiction: treatment and control in Britain*. Cambridge: Tavistock.

Waldorf D., Biernacki P. (1979) "Natural recovery from heroin addiction: a review of the incidence literature", *Journal of Drug Issues*, Spring.

Chapter 9: Drugs and the media

Bean P. (1993) "'Cocaine and crack: the promotion of an epidemic", *in* Bean, P. (*ed.*) *Cocaine and crack: supply and use*. Macmillan.

Gossop M. (1993) *Living with drugs. 3rd edition*. Aldershot: Ashgate.

Kohn M. (1987) *Narcomania: on heroin*. London: Faber and Faber.

Kohn M. (1992) *Dope Girls: The birth of the British underground*. London: Lawrence & Wishart.

Reeves J. L., Campbell R. (1994) *Cracked coverage: television news, the anti-cocaine crusade, and the Reagan legacy*. Durham: Duke University Press.

Chapter 10: Drug myths

Ditton J., Hammersley R. (1994) "The typical cocaine user", *Druglink*, November/December, ISDD.

Gabe J., Williams P. (*eds.*) (1986) *Tranquillisers: social, psychological and clinical perspectives*. London: Tavistock.

Gossop M. (1993) *Living with drugs. 3rd edition*. Cambridge: Arena.

Leitner M. *et al* (1993) *Drug usage and drugs prevention: the views and habits of the general public*. HMSO, London.

Tyler A. (1986) *Street drugs: the facts explained. The myths exploded*. (Revised edition, 1995). Suffolk: New English Library.

Index